Information Literacy Efforts
Benchmarks, 2013 Edition

ISBN: 978-1-57440-214-8
Library of Congress Control Number: 2012953149
© 2012 Primary Research Group, Inc.

Table of Contents

List of Tables

Survey Participants

Arkansas Tech University
Athens State University
Barstow College
Becker College
Berkeley City College
Blue Mountain Community College
Bowling Green State University – Firelands
California State University, East Bay
Central Pennsylvania College
Central Piedmont Community College
Charter College
Chesapeake College
Cleveland State University
Coastal Carolina University
Cochise College
College of Mount St. Joseph
Concordia College
Connors State College
Davenport University
Embry Riddle Aero University
Florida Keys Community College
Fox Valley Technical College
Frederick Community College
Georgia Southwestern State University
Lamar State College – Orange
Lewis Clark State College
Liberty University
Loyola University New Orleans
Meridian Community College
Michigan State University
Missouri Southern State University
Mott Community College
Northeast Lakeview College
Northwestern Michigan College
Nova Southeastern University
Oregon Institute of Technology
Pellissippi State University
Philadelphia University
Prairie View A&M University
Renton Technical College
Resurrection University
Richmond Community College
Riverside Community College

Roger Williams University
Sanford-Brown Institute – Jacksonville
Seneca College
South University
Southeastern University
Southern Utah University
Springfield Technical Community College
St. Charles Community College
Trinity Western University
University at Buffalo, SUNY
University of Columbus
University of Louisville
University of Notre Dame
University of Portland
University of Tampa
University of Wisconsin Superior
Western Connecticut State University

The Questionnaire

1. Please provide the following contact information
   Name:
   Organization:
   Work Title:
   Email Address:
   Country:

2. What is the current total full-time equivalent enrollment at your institution?

3. Which Carnegie Class best describes your college?
   (a) Community College
   (b) 4-Year College
   (c) MA or PHD Granting College
   (d) Research University

4. Is your college public or private?
   (a) Public
   (b) Private

5. Which statement best characterizes how your library uses library personnel for instructional purposes?
   (a) We have a staff dedicated to instruction that conducts most of the formal classes and devises or chooses most information literary materials
   (b) We have a staff largely dedicated to instruction but this is supplemented by librarians who also conduct classes
   (c) We have an education coordinator but not what I would call a real staff and the coordinator works with a broad range of librarians to conduct classes and choose materials

6. What is the total number of in-class instruction or presentation sessions given by the college's librarians in all classes in the past year?

7. For the fall semester of the 2012-13 academic year, what has been the approximate percentage change from the fall semester 2011-12 semester in the following areas?
   Number of Classes/Presentations Given:
   Number of Students Served Through Classes or Presentations:

8. In the last year, how many instructors gave a formal library instruction session or class presentation in any type of class?

9. Apart from the main college writing course, what are the three academic departments that requested the most library instructional presentations/classes in the past year?

10. In your view, about what percentage of students who have not taken any formal information literacy training know a few of the essentials of Boolean searching such as the use of quotation marks, use of "or", "and" or the +/- plus signs to focus searches?

11. How would you rate the information literacy skills of your student body in the following skill categories?

Ability to assess the credibility of information from websites
    (a) Highly proficient
    (b) Competent
    (c) Have a basic knowledge at best
    (d) Very unskilled

Knowledge of the basic concept of plagiarism and how to avoid it
    (a) Highly proficient
    (b) Competent
    (c) Have a basic knowledge at best
    (d) Very unskilled

Use of the online library catalog
    (a) Highly proficient
    (b) Competent
    (c) Have a basic knowledge at best
    (d) Very unskilled

Use of search engines
    (a) Highly proficient
    (b) Competent
    (c) Have a basic knowledge at best
    (d) Very unskilled

Use of periodicals databases
    (a) Highly proficient
    (b) Competent
    (c) Have a basic knowledge at best
    (d) Very unskilled

Use of e-book collections
    (a) Highly proficient
    (b) Competent
    (c) Have a basic knowledge at best
    (d) Very unskilled

Use of major databases
    (a) Highly proficient
    (b) Competent
    (c) Have a basic knowledge at best
    (d) Very unskilled

Use of library special collections
    (a) Highly proficient
    (b) Competent
    (c) Have a basic knowledge at best
    (d) Very unskilled

12. Has the college ever administered a test to assess student skills in any of the following areas?
    (a) Use of the college online catalog
    (b) Use of search engines and general web navigability
    (c) Use of Word, WordPerfect or other word processing software
    (d) Use of Excel or other spreadsheet software
    (e) Use of Windows

13. Does the library administer an information literacy test to incoming freshmen or transfers for any of the following skills? Select all that apply
    (a) Capacity to use periodicals databases
    (b) Capacity to use the online library catalog
    (c) Capabilities with search methodology
    (d) Understanding or plagiarism
    (e) Capacity to use e-book collections
    (f) Do not administer any tests

14. Is any form of information or computer literacy test required for graduation?
    (a) Yes
    (b) No
    (c) No, but we will probably adopt soon

15. Does the library use any of the following means to assess the performance of information literacy or other library science instructors? Select all that apply
    (a) Student evaluation forms
    (b) Videotaping or otherwise recording instruction sessions for later review
    (c) Senior librarians sit in on and evaluate library instruction classes
    (d) Student standardized test results

16. In the past year did the library administer to college faculty a library education services evaluation form to assess satisfaction with library assistance to faculty?
    (a) Yes
    (b) No

17. If the library has administered a library education services evaluation form to faculty in the past three years, how many did it distribute and how many did it get back (for the most recent period for which data is available)?

Distributed:

Received:

18. Does the library make presentations or give brief classes to new students during the new student orientation?

(a) Yes

(b) No

19. If the library makes presentations or gives classes to incoming students during their orientation, what is the average amount of time (in hours or fractions thereof) that the students spend in these library sessions during orientation?

20. Does the library participate in any kind of orientation or information literacy training class or period designed especially for distance learning students?

(a) Yes

(b) No

(c) Our college does not offer distance learning

21. Does the college require any of the following for graduation?

(a) A one or two credit information literacy course

(b) A three credit (or more) information literacy course

(c) Information literacy training integrated into basic writing or composition courses

(d) Information literacy integrated into basic courses in areas other than writing or composition

(e) No formal information literacy requirement

22. If your college does not have a formal information literacy course requirement, how likely is it than it will adopt one within the next three years?

(a) Unlikely

(b) It's possible but I would not say it's likely

(c) We have something in the pipeline and approval is likely

(d) We already have approval and will implement very soon

23. Does the college offer any online or distance learning information literacy courses?

(a) Yes

(b) No

24. Do any librarians currently serve on the college curriculum committee or its equivalent?

(a) Yes

(b) No

25. Does the library offer any information literacy courses that are cross listed (offered by both) with other departments, such as computer science, psychology, history, biology, etc, or schools, such as a medical or law school?
    (a) Yes
    (b) No

26. Which phrase best describes the attitude of upper college administrative management towards information literacy?
    (a) I am afraid that it is not high on their agenda
    (b) They sometimes pay attention and sometime not
    (c) It is increasingly a high priority
    (d) It is a high priority for the college

26. Do librarians at your institution have faculty status?
    (a) Yes
    (b) No

27. Does the library send library science instructors to teach sessions to students taking the college's main English composition, rhetoric or similar required course?
    (a) Yes
    (b) No

28. To what degree do library instructors make appearances in the basic composition class?
    (a) A predetermined set number of appearances
    (b) Pretty much determined by the English Department
    (c) Pretty much determined by individual composition instructors

29. In approximately how many three credit composition classes do library instructors make an appearance per semester?

30. What is your attitude towards how the English Department (or equivalent department with similar responsibilities) carries out its information literacy responsibilities?
    (a) Honestly we feel that they are somewhat laggard
    (b) They seem to try but they could do better
    (c) They do well enough
    (d) It is a high propriety for them and they make time for us
    (e) I consider it an excellent collaboration and we jointly accomplish our information literacy goals

31. Does the college offer interactive tutorials in information literacy topics to students?
    (a) Yes
    (b) No

32. If the college does offer interactive tutorials in information literacy topics to students, how many such tutorials are currently offered?

33. Does the college offer video tutorials on information literacy topics?
   (a) Yes
   (b) No

34. What has been the library's experience in using and making online or video-based tutorials for information literacy? Do you make your own or use those of other colleges or both? What kind of software or websites do you use to help you to make the videos or online tutorials? How do you market and distribute them?

35. If the library offers interactive tutorials over the web, approximately how many unique visits does the tutorial page receive on a typical month when college is in session?

36. Does the library have one or more instructional labs or learning centers designed for information literacy instruction in which much of the library's formal information literacy instruction takes place?
   (a) Yes
   (b) No

37. If the library has such a center or centers, how many seats or individual workstations do these centers offer in total? Add up the seats for all centers designed specifically for use by the library for education projects.

38. What percentage of the time when college is in full session is the center in use by any party including by non-library instructors?

39. How many years ago was the center constructed or significantly remodeled, defined as refurbishing or re-equipping at a cost of greater than one third of initial outlays for all equipment and construction or a cost greater than $25,000?

40. Which phrase best describes the level of investment in equipment, space, software and other aids to teach information literacy and related subjects the library will makes over the next three years?
   (a) Increase significantly relative to the recent past
   (b) Increase somewhat
   (c) Remain about the same
   (d) Be reduced somewhat; we have made our major investments or do not plan to
   (e) Decline precipitously

41. Please mention some of the resources that you have used in designing and maintaining your information literacy program. Please mention valued websites, listservs, blogs, books, monographs, journals, databases, tutorials, newsletters, magazines, e-zines, conferences and other favored resources.

42. What role have social media sites such as Twitter and Facebook and video aggregation sites (such as YouTube and Vimeo) played in your information literacy efforts?

Summary of Main Findings

Staffing

48.21% of college libraries in the sample have a staff dedicated to instruction that conducts most information literacy classes and selects related class materials, including 57.14% of community college libraries, 58.82% of 4-year college libraries and 33.33% of libraries in MA and PHD granting colleges. 16.07% of college libraries have a staff dedicated to information literacy instruction but supplement this staff with librarians who also conduct classes, whereas 35.71% have an education coordinator who works with a broad range of librarians to conduct classes and choose materials.

100% of research university libraries have a staff largely dedicated to instruction which they supplement with librarians who also conduct information literacy classes, as do 31.58% of colleges with more than 5,000 students enrolled but just 5.88% of those with less than 2,500 students. 47.06% of the latter have a staff dedicated to instruction which conducts most classes and chooses most information literacy materials and the same percentage have an education coordinator who works with a number of librarians to conduct classes. In general, libraries in the sample that have had more than 100 instruction or presentation sessions given by college librarians in the last year tend to rely more on staffs of dedicated instructors than on education coordinators who work with college librarians.

In the last year, a mean of 8.68 instructors in college libraries in the sample gave a formal library instruction session or class presentation of some kind. A mean of 30.5 instructors in research universities taught a library instruction session, compared with a mean of 6.67 instructors in community colleges, 6.88 instructors in MA and PHD granting colleges and 10.65 instructors in 4-year colleges. Public colleges in the sample relied on a mean of 7.67 instructors to give formal library instruction sessions last year, whereas private colleges had a mean of 10.65 different instructors. Unsurprisingly, college libraries with the most students enrolled and those which administered the most instruction sessions tend to have more information literacy instructors than those with fewer students and fewer instruction sessions.

Classes and Presentations

Libraries in the sample have given 22.82% more information literacy classes and presentations in the fall 2012-13 semester than they gave in the fall 2011-12 semester. Public colleges increased the number of these classes by a mean of 28.6%, while private colleges increased them by a mean of 10.5%. Community colleges gave 13.74% more information literacy classes in the fall of 2012-13, 4-year colleges gave a mean of 32.93% more classes and MA and PHD granting colleges increased the number of classes by a mean of 24.54%. Whereas colleges with less than 2,500 students enrolled gave 14.84% more information literacy classes and presentations than in the previous year, colleges with 2,500 to 5,000 students gave a mean of 20.19% more classes and those with over 5,000 students gave about 31.88% more classes.

A mean of 26.09% more students will be served through information literacy classes and presentations in the fall 2012-13 semester than in the fall 2011-12 semester, though some college libraries will serve fewer students this year than in the year prior. Public college libraries will serve 36.3% more students through information literacy classes, while private college libraries will serve a mean of 7.36% more students. College libraries with more than 5,000 students will serve 26.29% more students, even as colleges which give more than 200 instruction sessions will increase the number of students served through these classes by a mean of just 3.57%.

Boolean Search Methods

Survey participants estimate that a mean of 15.56% of students who have not had any formal information training know a few of the essentials of Boolean searching, such as the use of quotation marks or the use of "and" or "or" to focus searches. Survey participants in community colleges expect just 10.86% of their students to be aware of these essentials, whereas those in 4-year colleges estimate that 21.93% of students have this knowledge. Survey participants in public colleges believe that 14.57% of students in their college know a few of the essentials of Boolean searching, while those in private colleges say that a mean of 17.61% of their students do. Survey participants in colleges with more than 5,000 students enrolled estimate that a mean of 21.1% of their students know some of the essentials of Boolean searching, while those in colleges with less than 2,500 students estimate that 10.65% of their students have this knowledge.

Ability to Assess the Credibility of Information

51.67% of survey participants feel that students at their college have a basic knowledge of how to assess the credibility of information from websites and 18.33% say that their students are competent in this area. 30% of survey participants say that their student body is very unskilled in assessing the credibility of information on the internet, most of these survey participants in community colleges, 54.17% of which say that their students are unskilled in this area. On the other hand, 75% of survey participants in MA and PHD granting colleges and 64.71% of those in 4-year colleges feel that their students have a basic knowledge of how to assess the credibility of information from websites, though none believe their students are highly proficient.

Knowledge of Plagiarism

20% of survey participants believe that their students have a competent knowledge of the basic concept of plagiarism and how to avoid and 63.33% say that they have a basic knowledge, while 15% of participants feel that their students are very unskilled in this regard. 1.67 % of survey participants feel that students in their college are highly proficient in their knowledge of plagiarism, all of these in private colleges with total student enrollment in excess of 5,000. 29.41% of survey participants in 4-year colleges and 33.33% of those in research universities rate their students as competent when it comes to plagiarism. Participants in community colleges are less confident, 62.5% saying their students have a basic understanding and 29.17% saying that they are very unskilled.

In general, survey participants in colleges with smaller student enrollments and fewer instruction sessions feel that their students have a better understanding of plagiarism than do those in larger colleges with more sessions.

Use of the Online Library Catalogue

In terms of their ability to use the online library catalogue, 51.67% of survey participants feel that their students have a basic knowledge and 26.67% feel that they are competent. 21.67% of survey participants consider their students very unskilled in this area, including 25% of survey participants in public colleges and 15% of those in private colleges. 71.43% of survey participants in colleges that have had 100 to 200 instruction sessions given by college librarians in the past year say that their students have a basic knowledge of the online library catalogue, along with 45.83% of participants in community colleges and the majority of those in 4-year colleges, MA and PHD granting colleges and research universities.

Use of Search Engines

41.67% of survey participants consider their students competent in the use of search engines and 1.67% consider them highly proficient, though these are limited to participants in public 4-year colleges with more than 5,000 students enrolled. 50% of survey participants in MA and PHD granting colleges and 47.06% of those in 4-year colleges rate their students as competent in this regard, while 58.33% of participants in community colleges and two-thirds of those in research universities say that their students have a basic knowledge. In total, 6.67% of survey participants believe that students at their college are very unskilled at using search engines, including 9.52% of participants in colleges with more than 5,000 students and 5.56% of those in colleges with less than 2,500 students.

Use of Periodicals Databases and E-Book Collections

When it comes to periodicals databases, 38.33% of survey participants say that students in their college are very unskilled and 48.33% say that they have a basic knowledge. Just 10% of survey participants believe that their students are competent in using periodicals databases and 3.33% rate their students highly proficient. Among those that consider their students very unskilled are 45.83% of survey participants in community colleges, 44.44% of participants in colleges with fewer than 2,500 students enrolled and 42.5% of survey participants in public colleges. 33.33% of survey participants in research universities believe that their students are competent in this regard, as do 5.88% of participants in 4-year colleges and 12.5% of participants in MA and PHD granting colleges.

Students are even less capable using e-book collections, with 54.24% of survey participants saying that their students are very unskilled in this area and 37.29% saying that they have a basic knowledge. 12.5% of survey participants in 4-year colleges and the same percentage of those in MA and PHD granting colleges consider their students competent with e-book collections, but these are the exceptions and not the rule. 64.71%

of survey participants in college consider their students very unskilled in the use of e-book collections, along with 42.86% of survey participants in colleges with 2,500 to 5,000 students and 57.14% of participants in colleges with more than 5,000 students.

Use of Major Databases

3.33% of survey participants consider students at their college highly proficient in the use of major databases, while 21.67% rate students as competent and 41.67% say that they have a basic knowledge. A third of survey participants consider their students very unskilled with major databases, 37.5% of participants in public colleges and 25% of those in private colleges. 66.67% of survey participants in research universities consider their students competent in this area, as do 31.25% of those in MA and PHD granting colleges but just 11.76% of participants in 4-year colleges. 58.82% of survey participants in the latter group say that their students have a basic knowledge of major databases and 5.88% say that they are highly proficient, whereas 45.83% of participants in community colleges rate their students as very unskilled.

Use of Library Special Collections

Use of library special collections is one of the areas in which students could use the most instruction, as 67.24% of survey participants consider their students unskilled in using these collections and just 1.72% see them as competent, all of these in public community colleges with more than 5,000 students enrolled. 75% of survey participants in colleges with 2,500 to 5,000 students enrolled, 75% of participants in colleges that have offered 100 to 200 instruction sessions given by college librarians in the past year and more than 81% of those in MA and PHD granting colleges say that their students are very unskilled in this area. 4-year colleges are among the brighter spots in the survey in this regard, with 43.75% of survey participants in these colleges saying that their students have a basic knowledge of library special collections.

Student Testing and Assessment

One-fourth of colleges in the sample have at one time administered tests to assess student skills in the use of the college's online catalogue. These include 37.5% of MA and PHD granting colleges, 33.33% of research universities and 25% of community colleges, but just 11.76% of 4-year colleges. 20% of colleges have given tests to assess student skills in the use of search engines and general web navigability, including 42.86% of those with more than 5,000 students currently enrolled. 25% of MA and PHD granting colleges and 33.33% of research universities have administered such tests, more than twice the percentage of community colleges which did the same.

Tests assessing student skills in the use of Word, WordPerfect or other word processing software have been administered by 16.67% of colleges in the sample, though none of these have been research universities. 12.5% of public colleges and 25% of private colleges have administered tests to students to assess their word processing skills, many of these colleges with student enrollments of less than 2,500, a third of which have given a test of this kind. Even fewer colleges have administered tests to assess student skills in the use of Excel or other spreadsheet software, 22.22% of colleges with less than 2,500 students enrolled and just 11.67% of colleges in total, and only 10% have administered tests to assess student skills in the use of Windows.

15% of colleges in the sample have some form of information or computer literacy examination that is required for student graduation and another 13.33% are considering implementing such an examination soon. 23.81% of colleges with more than 5,000 students have an information literacy test that is required for graduation, as do 16.67% of colleges with less than 2,500 students, an additional 22.22% of which will probably implement one soon. 12.5% of community colleges have an information literacy exam required for graduation and 16.67% hope to adopt one soon, compared with 33.33% of research universities and 6.25% of MA and PHD granting colleges.

Testing Incoming Freshmen and Transfers

Information literacy tests of some kind are administered to freshmen and/or transfer students in 24.07% of colleges in the sample; many of these are MA and PHD granting colleges, 42.86% of which administer information literacy tests to incoming students, but they also include 13.04% of community colleges, 21.43% of 4-year colleges and a third of research universities. 36.84% of colleges with more than 5,000 students enrolled and the same percentage of those which offered 100 to 200 instruction sessions given by college librarians in the past year administered information literacy tests to incoming freshmen and transfer students.

20.37% of colleges in the sample have administered tests to freshman and transfer students to assess their capacity to use periodicals databases and the same percentage have tested these students' ability to use the online library catalogue. 13.04% of community colleges, 14.29% of 4-year colleges, 35.71% of MA and PHD granting colleges and 33.33% of administered tests to incoming students to assess each of these skills. These tests have also been given by 17.65% of colleges with less than 2,500 students enrolled and 36.84% of colleges with over 5,000 students enrolled.

Incoming freshman and transfer students are tested for their capabilities with search methodology by 18.52% of colleges in the sample and for an understanding of plagiarism by 12.96% of colleges in the sample. Just 4.35% of community colleges administered tests to students for their capabilities with search methodology, while 21.43% of 4-year colleges and 35.71% of MA and PHD granting colleges did the same. Whereas 31.58% of colleges with more than 5,000 students tested freshman and transfer students for their skills with search methodology, about 21.05% of colleges in this same group and 0% of those with 2,500 to 5,000 students tested students for their understanding of plagiarism.

Evaluating Faculty Performance

Student evaluation forms are used by 61.67% of colleges in the sample, including the majority of community, 4-year and MA and PHD granting colleges, to assess the performance of information literacy or other library science instructors. 18.33% of colleges in the sample use student standardized test results to assess the performance of information literacy instructors. These include 29.41% of 4-year colleges, 27.78% of colleges with less than 2,500 students enrolled and 23.81% of colleges that have offered less than 200 information literacy instruction sessions in the past year.

Just 3.33% of colleges videotape or record information literacy instruction sessions for later review, all of these public colleges with 2,500 to 5,000 students enrolled. 10% of colleges have senior librarians sit in on and evaluate library instruction classes, 12.5% of public colleges and 5% of private colleges. 4.17% of community colleges, 17.65% of 4-year colleges and 12.5% of MA and PHD granting colleges have senior librarians sit it on library instruction classes.

In the past year, 31.67% of colleges in the sample have administered library education services evaluation forms to faculty members to assess satisfaction with library assistance to faculty. 33.33% of community colleges and the same percentage of research universities have administered library education services evaluation forms to faculty, along with 29.45% of 4-year colleges and 31.25% of MA and PHD granting colleges. These colleges distributed a mean of 464.44 such evaluation forms and maximum of 6,000, but only received a mean of 109.65 and a maximum of 915. 3.57 – 3.89

New Student Orientation

52.5% of public college libraries and 65% of private college libraries make presentations or give classes to new students during the new student orientation, together accounting for 56.67% of college libraries in the sample. Colleges with fewer students enrolled are somewhat more likely to include library presentations or classes in new student orientation than those with more students; 61.11% of libraries with fewer than 2,500 students enrolled in their college give brief classes or presentations during orientation, as compared to 52.38% of libraries in colleges with more than 5,000 students. 76.47% of 4-year college libraries give these classes or presentations, as do 56.25% of MA and PHD granting college libraries and 45.83% of community college libraries.

Among colleges in the sample, library sessions given during new student orientation last a mean of 0.66 hours (40 minutes) and a maximum of 1.5 hours (90 minutes). These sessions are shortest in research universities, where they last a mean of just 0.2 hours (12 minutes) and longest in MA and PHD granting colleges, where they take up a mean of 0.84 hours (50 minutes).

41.67% of college libraries participate in some kind of orientation or information literacy training class designed especially for online or distance learning students, including 56.25% of MA and PHD granting college libraries and 37.5% of libraries in community colleges. 37.5% of public college libraries and 50% of private college libraries have an orientation or information literacy training class specifically for distance learning students. The same is true of 50% of college libraries that offered more than 200 instruction sessions given by college librarians in the past year.

Course Requirements and Offerings

28.33% of colleges in the sample have a formal information literacy requirement for graduation, including 38.89% of colleges with less than 2,500 students enrolled, but less than 15% of those with 2,500 to 5,000 students. 5% of colleges in the sample require a one or two credit information literacy course for graduation, these limited to a small percentage of public 4-year and MA and PHD granting colleges, and none require a three or more credit course. Most colleges in the sample prefer to incorporate information literacy training into other required courses; 13.33% integrate this training into basic writing and composition courses and 16.67% integrate it into other non-writing required courses.

As many as 20.83% of community colleges and 12.5% of MA and PHD granting colleges require information literacy training integrated into basic writing or composition courses, though just 5.88% of 4-year colleges and no research universities have a similar requirement. In comparison, 29.41% of 4-year colleges, 12.5% of community colleges and the same percentage of MA and PHD granting colleges integrate this training into basic non-writing courses. Many of these are colleges with less than 2,500 students enrolled, nearly 39% of which require this training in basic non-writing courses. 35% of private colleges in the sample require information literacy training integrated into basic courses in areas other than writing and composition, whereas just 7.5% of public colleges do the same.

55.56% of colleges that administered less than 100 information literacy instruction sessions in the past year and which do not impose a formal information literacy course requirement are unlikely to adopt such a requirement in the next three years, whereas the majority of those that administered more than 100 instruction sessions consider it a possibility. In total, 28.57% of survey participants in colleges without information literacy course requirements feel it is unlikely that their college will adopt this requirement, 59.18% feel it is possible but not likely, 8.16% say that they have something in the pipeline and that approval is likely and 4.08% say that they already have approval and will be implementing this requirement soon.

Online and distance learning information literacy courses are offered by 26.67% of colleges in the sample, most of these public colleges, 32.5% of which offer courses of this kind. 37.5% of MA and PHD granting colleges and 29.17% of community colleges offer information literacy courses online, though just 11.76% of 4-year colleges do the same. 38.1% of colleges with more than 5,000 students enrolled offer online or distance learning information literacy courses, twice the percentage of colleges with 2,500 to 5,000 students and considerably more than the 22.22% of colleges with less than 2,500 students that do so.

Power and Influence

In 71.67% of colleges in the sample, 75% of public colleges and 65% of private colleges, librarians serve on the college curriculum committee or its equivalent. 56.67% of colleges in the sample give librarians faculty status, including 41.67% of community colleges, 47.06% of 4-year colleges, 81.25% of MA and PHD granting colleges and 100% of research universities. 38.89% of colleges with less than 2,500 students enrolled offer librarians faculty status, along with 71.43% of colleges with 2,500 to 5,000 students and 57.14% of colleges with more than 5,000 students.

7.5% of public college libraries and 30% of private college libraries offer information literacy courses that are cross listed with other departments and/or schools. 4.17% of community college libraries, 17.65% of 4-year college libraries, 18.75% of MA and PHD granting college libraries and 66.67% of research university libraries offer courses cross listed with other departments, together accounting for 15% of libraries in the sample. While 33.33% of libraries in colleges with student enrollments of more than 5,000 offer information literacy courses cross listed with other departments, just 5.56% of those with fewer than 2,500 students and less than 5% of those with 2,500 to 5,000 students do so.

Just 5% of survey participants feel that upper college administrators consider information literacy a high priority, though 16.67% say it is increasingly becoming a priority. 46.67% of survey participants say that upper level administrators sometimes pay attention to information literacy efforts and 31.67% say that it is not high on their agenda. This frustration is most palpable among survey participants in research universities, 66.67% of which believe information literacy is not high on administrators' list of priorities, and among those in MA and PHD granting colleges, 37.5% of which also feel this way. At the same time, 14.29% of survey participants in colleges with 2,500 to 5,000 students enrolled and 23.81% of participants in colleges with more than 5,000 students say that information literacy is increasingly becoming a high priority for their college.

Relations with the English Department

84.21% of colleges in the sample send library science instructors to teach sessions to students taking the college's main English composition, rhetoric or similar required course. These include 93.33% of MA and PHD granting colleges, 82.61% of community colleges, 81.25% of 4-year colleges and 66.67% of research universities. 87.18% of public colleges send library science instructors to teach sessions to students in the college's main composition or rhetoric course, as opposed to 77.78% of private colleges.

In 72.73% of colleges in the sample the number of appearances made by college librarians in basic composition classes is determined by the individual class instructor, while in 12.73% of colleges it is determined by the English Department as a whole and in 14.55% of colleges it is predetermined by the college. Colleges with fewer students and which offer less information literacy presentation or instruction sessions are considerably more likely to leave the number of appearances by college librarians in basic composition classes up to the instructors themselves; 31.25% of colleges with more than 5,000 students have librarians make a predetermined number of appearances, compared with 6.25% of colleges with less than 2,500 students.

Library instructors in colleges in the sample make a mean of 21.95 appearances in three credit composition classes per semester, about 27.65 appearances in public colleges and a mean of 8.35 appearances in private colleges. In 4-year colleges library instructors make somewhat more appearances in three credit composition classes, a mean of 29.67 per semester compared with 18.95 appearances in community colleges and 19.36 appearances in MA and PHD granting colleges. They also make somewhat more appearances in larger colleges, a mean of 37.2 among those with more than 5,000 students enrolled.

Survey participants have mixed opinions about how well the English Department carries out its information literacy responsibilities. 10.34% of participants feel that their English Department is laggard in this regard and 39.66% say that they try but could do better, while 12.07% of survey participants believe that their English Department does well enough and 37.93% have more positive feedback. Among the least satisfied are survey participants in community colleges, 16.67% of which say that their English Department is laggard, and participants in MA and PHD granting colleges, 46.67% of which feel that their department could do better. 32.5% of survey participants in public colleges believe that information literacy is a high priority for their English Department, while 61.11% of those in private colleges say that they seem to try but could do better.

Interactive and Video Tutorials

Interactive tutorials in information literacy topics are offered to students by 47.46% of libraries in the sample, 40% of public colleges and 63.16% of private ones. Nearly 62% of colleges with more than 2,500 students enrolled offer interactive tutorials in information literacy, whereas 38.89% of colleges with less than 2,500 students and 40% of those with 2,500 to 5,000 students offer tutorials of this kind. 100% of research universities offer interactive tutorials in information literacy, along with 37.5% of community colleges, 52.94% of 4-year colleges and 46.67% of MA and PHD granting colleges.

On average, colleges that have interactive tutorials in information literacy topics offer a mean of 6.81 different tutorials of this kind. MA and PHD granting colleges offer a mean of 9.71 such tutorials and a maximum of 20, while community colleges offer a mean of 5.67 and 4-year colleges offer a mean of 5.13. Libraries in the sample that offer interactive tutorials over the web receive a mean of 1,184 unique visits to their tutorial page in a typical month while college is in session, though this number is skewed dramatically by a single outlier that receives 10,000 unique visits per month. Public college libraries get a mean of 148 unique visits to their tutorial page, while private college libraries receive a mean of 2,220 unique visits and a median of 50.

Video tutorials on information literacy topics are offered by 65.52% of college libraries in the sample, including 75% of those in 4-year colleges and the majority of those in community colleges and MA and PHD granting colleges. 61.9% of libraries that offered less than 100 instruction sessions given by college librarians in the past year offer students video tutorials, as did 75% of those than offered 100 to 200 instruction sessions and 58.82% of those that offered more than 200 sessions..

Instructional Labs

55.93% of college libraries in the sample have one or more instructional labs or learning centers designed for information literacy instruction in which most of the library's information literacy efforts take place. 66.67% of MA and PHD granting college libraries and the same percentage of research university libraries have an instructional lab where most of the formal information literacy instruction occurs, as do 58.33% of community college libraries and 41.83% of 4-year college libraries. 65% of public college libraries have an instructional lab of this kind, compared with 36.84% of private college libraries. 72.22% of colleges that had more than 200 instruction sessions given by college librarians have one or more instructional labs for information literacy instruction, while 38.1% of those that offered fewer than 100 instruction sessions have a facility of this kind.

Among libraries in the sample, instructional labs or learning centers as described above offer a mean of 42.6 total seats or individual workstations. Instructional labs in community college libraries seat a mean of 29.53 students, while those in research universities seat a mean of 128.5 and a minimum of 100 students. These labs are in use a mean of 48.13% of the time while the college is in full session, 49.6% of the time in public colleges and 42.86% of the time in private colleges. On average, instructional labs designed for information literacy instruction in colleges in the sample were constructed or remodeled about 6.43 years ago, though some colleges have not significantly remodeled in 16 years. Colleges with less than 2,500 students remodeled a mean of 8.43 years ago, while those with more than 5,000 students remodeled a mean of 5.56 years ago.

14.55% of libraries in the sample plan to significantly increase the level of investment in equipment, space, software and other aids to teach information literacy and related subjects over the next three years and 29.09% plan to increase investment somewhat. Just 5.46% of college libraries will reduce their level of investment in this area and these are limited to public community and 4-year colleges. 25% of private college libraries plan to increase their investment in information literacy equipment and space, whereas just 10.26% of public college libraries will do the same. 4-year colleges and MA and PHD granting colleges are among those that will most increase investment in this area, while 56.52% of community colleges and 100% of research universities will keep their level of investment about the same.

Characteristics of the Sample

Type of College

	Community College	4-Year College	MA or PHD Granting College	Research University
Entire Sample	40.00%	28.33%	26.67%	5.00%

Public or Private Status

	Public	Private
Entire Sample	66.67%	33.33%

Total Student Enrollment (FTE)

	Less than 2,500	2,500 to 5,000	More than 5,000
Entire Sample	30.00%	35.00%	35.00%

Total Number of Instruction or Presentation Sessions given by the College's Librarians in All Classes in the Past Year

	Less than 100	100 to 200	More than 200
Entire Sample	35.00%	35.00%	30.00%

Chapter 1: Staffing and Budgeting

Table 1.1: Which statement best characterizes how your library uses library personnel for instructional purposes?

	We have a staff dedicated to instruction that conducts most of the classes and chooses most information literacy materials	We have a staff largely dedicated to instruction but they are supplemented by librarians who also conduct classes	We have an education coordinator who works with a broad range of librarians to conduct classes and choose materials
Entire Sample	48.21%	16.07%	35.71%

Table 1.2: Which statement best characterizes how your library uses library personnel for instructional purposes? Broken Out by Type of College

Type of College	We have a staff dedicated to instruction that conducts most of the classes and chooses most information literacy materials	We have a staff largely dedicated to instruction but they are supplemented by librarians who also conduct classes	We have an education coordinator who works with a broad range of librarians to conduct classes and choose materials
Community College	57.14%	4.76%	38.10%
4-Year College	58.82%	11.76%	29.41%
MA or PHD Granting College	33.33%	20.00%	46.67%
Research University	0.00%	100.00%	0.00%

Table 1.3: Which statement best characterizes how your library uses library personnel for instructional purposes? Broken Out by Public or Private Status

Public or Private Status	We have a staff dedicated to instruction that conducts most of the classes and chooses most information literacy materials	We have a staff largely dedicated to instruction but they are supplemented by librarians who also conduct classes	We have an education coordinator who works with a broad range of librarians to conduct classes and choose materials
Public	55.56%	16.67%	27.78%
Private	35.00%	15.00%	50.00%

Table 1.4:   Which statement best characterizes how your library uses library personnel for instructional purposes? Broken Out by Total Student Enrollment

Total Student Enrollment	We have a staff dedicated to instruction that conducts most of the classes and chooses most information literacy materials	We have a staff largely dedicated to instruction but they are supplemented by librarians who also conduct classes	We have an education coordinator who works with a broad range of librarians to conduct classes and choose materials
Less than 2,500	47.06%	5.88%	47.06%
2,500 to 5,000	50.00%	10.00%	40.00%
More than 5,000	47.37%	31.58%	21.05%

Table 1.5:   Which statement best characterizes how your library uses library personnel for instructional purposes? Broken Out by Total Number of Instruction or Presentation Sessions given by the College's Librarians in the Past Year

Number of Instruction Sessions given by College Librarians	We have a staff dedicated to instruction that conducts most of the classes and chooses most information literacy materials	We have a staff largely dedicated to instruction but they are supplemented by librarians who also conduct classes	We have an education coordinator who works with a broad range of librarians to conduct classes and choose materials
Less than 100	47.06%	5.88%	47.06%
100 to 200	47.62%	19.05%	33.33%
More than 200	50.00%	22.22%	27.78%

Table 1.6:   What has been the approximate percentage change in the number of classes/presentations given from the fall 2011-12 semester to the fall 2012-13 semester?

	Mean	Median	Minimum	Maximum
Entire Sample	22.82	9.00	-25.00	163.00

Table 1.7: **What has been the approximate percentage change in the number of classes/presentations given from the fall 2011-12 semester to the fall 2012-13 semester? Broken Out by Type of College**

Type of College	Mean	Median	Minimum	Maximum
Community College	13.74	1.40	-12.00	86.00
4-Year College	32.93	12.00	-13.00	150.00
MA or PHD Granting College	24.54	9.50	-25.00	163.00
Research University	42.50	42.50	42.50	42.50

Table 1.8: **What has been the approximate percentage change in the number of classes/presentations given from the fall 2011-12 semester to the fall 2012-13 semester? Broken Out by Public or Private Status**

Public or Private Status	Mean	Median	Minimum	Maximum
Public	28.60	9.50	-13.00	163.00
Private	10.50	9.00	-25.00	61.00

Table 1.9: **What has been the approximate percentage change in the number of classes/presentations given from the fall 2011-12 semester to the fall 2012-13 semester? Broken Out by Total Student Enrollment**

Total Student Enrollment	Mean	Median	Minimum	Maximum
Less than 2,500	14.84	7.50	-12.00	61.00
2,500 to 5,000	20.19	9.50	-25.00	144.00
More than 5,000	31.88	9.00	-13.00	163.00

Table 1.10: **What has been the approximate percentage change in the number of classes/presentations given from the fall 2011-12 semester to the fall 2012-13 semester? Broken Out by Total Number of Instruction or Presentation Sessions given by the College's Librarians in the Past Year**

Number of Instruction Sessions given by College Librarians	Mean	Median	Minimum	Maximum
Less than 100	18.47	10.00	-9.50	100.00
100 to 200	28.04	13.50	-25.00	150.00
More than 200	20.78	0.50	-13.00	163.00

Table 1.11:   What has been the approximate percentage change in the number of students served through classes or presentations from the fall 2011-12 semester to the fall 2012-13 semester?

	Mean	Median	Minimum	Maximum
Entire Sample	26.09	5.00	-17.00	150.00

Table 1.12:   What has been the approximate percentage change in the number of students served through classes or presentations from the fall 2011-12 semester to the fall 2012-13 semester? Broken Out by Public or Private Status

Public or Private Status	Mean	Median	Minimum	Maximum
Public	36.63	12.50	-10.00	150.00
Private	7.36	5.00	-17.00	33.00

Table 1.13:   What has been the approximate percentage change in the number of students served through classes or presentations from the fall 2011-12 semester to the fall 2012-13 semester? Broken Out by Total Student Enrollment

Total Student Enrollment	Mean	Median	Minimum	Maximum
Less than 2,500	26.29	10.00	-17.00	111.00
2,500 to 5,000	16.30	4.50	-10.00	101.00
More than 5,000	38.16	19.00	-3.75	150.00

Table 1.14:   What has been the approximate percentage change in the number of students served through classes or presentations from the fall 2011-12 semester to the fall 2012-13 semester? Broken Out by Total Number of Instruction or Presentation Sessions given by the College's Librarians in the Past Year

Number of Instruction Sessions given by College Librarians	Mean	Median	Minimum	Maximum
Less than 100	39.43	10.00	0.00	111.00
100 to 200	31.93	20.00	-3.75	150.00
More than 200	3.57	4.00	-17.00	25.00

*Not enough information to calculate the percentage change in the number of students served through classes or presentations from the fall 2011-12 semester to the fall 2012-13 semester broken out by type of college

Table 1.15:   In the last year, how many instructors gave a formal library instruction session or class presentation in any type of class?

	Mean	Median	Minimum	Maximum
Entire Sample	8.68	4.00	0.00	71.00

Table 1.16:   In the last year, how many instructors gave a formal library instruction session or class presentation in any type of class? Broken Out by Type of College

Type of College	Mean	Median	Minimum	Maximum
Community College	6.67	3.00	0.00	38.00
4-Year College	10.65	5.00	1.00	71.00
MA or PHD Granting College	6.88	7.50	2.00	15.00
Research University	30.50	30.50	11.00	50.00

Table 1.17:   In the last year, how many instructors gave a formal library instruction session or class presentation in any type of class? Broken Out by Public or Private Status

Public or Private Status	Mean	Median	Minimum	Maximum
Public	7.67	4.00	0.00	71.00
Private	10.65	5.50	1.00	50.00

Table 1.18:   In the last year, how many instructors gave a formal library instruction session or class presentation in any type of class? Broken Out by Total Student Enrollment

Total Student Enrollment	Mean	Median	Minimum	Maximum
Less than 2,500	4.89	3.00	1.00	27.00
2,500 to 5,000	7.62	4.00	1.00	38.00
More than 5,000	13.20	8.50	0.00	71.00

Table 1.19:   In the last year, how many instructors gave a formal library instruction session or class presentation in any type of class? Broken Out by Total Number of Instruction or Presentation Sessions given by the College's Librarians in the Past Year

Number of Instruction Sessions given by College Librarians	Mean	Median	Minimum	Maximum
Less than 100	5.52	2.00	0.00	34.00
100 to 200	8.50	4.50	2.00	71.00
More than 200	12.56	8.00	3.00	50.00

Apart from the main college writing course, what are the three academic departments that requested the most library instructional presentations/classes in the past year?

1. College Success course, Humanities
2. Health Science, Counseling, Social Science
3. Department of Communications, School of Engineering
4. Business, Education, Psychology
5. Communication, History, Business
6. English, Speech, Education
7. English, Speech, Business
8. College Survival Skills, Criminal Justice, Psychology
9. Biology, Psychology, and Education
10. Nursing, Humanities, and Reading
11. Nursing, Speech Communication, Education/Psychology (tied)
12. Sociology, Nursing, Speech
13. Nursing, Media & Marketing, Early Childhood Education
14. English (upper level classes, in addition to basic), Reading, Government
15. Business, Education, Social Sciences
16. Educational Leadership, Social Work, Psychology
17. General Studies, Health Professions, Legal
18. College of General Studies, Education, and History
19. Allied Health/Nursing, Biology, Engineering
20. Speech, College Skills, Literature
21. Graduate Theology, Undergraduate Communication, Graduate Nursing
22. Psychology, Freshman Seminar Course (our 1st-year intro, every class has a information lit session), Communications
23. Biology, English, Education
24. Medical Assisting, General Education, Criminal Justice
25. First Year Experience, Nursing, Biology
26. Nursing, Veterinary Medicine, Pharmacy
27. College Experience, History, Business
28. Humanities/Communications, Global Safety & Information Security, UNIV 101 (introductory freshman class)
29. Nursing, Communications
30. Religious Studies, Mass Communication, Sociology
31. English Literature, Nursing
32. Nursing, Dental, Occupational Therapy
33. Business, Teacher Education, Psychology

34. Mechanical Engineering, Civil Engineering
35. Architecture, Fashion, Health Sciences
36. College Success Initiative (class for all freshman), Speech, Nursing, Computer Science
37. World Civilizations
38. Nursing, Economics, Geography
39. Communications, Academic Success, English
40. Communications, Academic/College Success Skills, Drama
41. English Department is first. Beyond that, there are a number of departments that are about even - Psychology, Geology/Environmental Studies, History, Political Science and Music.
42. Business, Justice Studies and Psychology
43. Developmental Education, Business, Health
44. Student Services and Research Departments
45. English, Psychology, History
46. College of Business, College of Arts & Letters programs
47. Public Speaking, Education, Health Science
48. Colleges of Pharmacy, Education, Optometry
49. English, Sociology, Education
50. Humanities, Social Sciences, Natural Sciences
51. Music, Education, Communications
52. General studies with the intro to college courses by far (college experience, freshman seminar, college success seminar), but also Biology105 & Psych 100 faculty requested sessions. Legal Studies would be the other department.
53. Theology, Nursing, Business
54. Freshman Year required course, Education, Business
55. English as Second Language, Allied Health/Nursing
56. Library tutorials were given to English, Orientation, and Geology/Physical Sciences, among others
57. Business, History, Psychology
58. Social Work, Business, Education
59. Psychology, Criminal Justice, Nursing

Chapter 2: Assessment of Pre-Instruction State of Information Literacy

Table 2.1: In your view, about what percentage of students who have not taken any formal information literacy training know a few of the essentials of Boolean searching such as the use of quotation marks, use of "or", "and" or the +/- plus signs to focus searches?

	Mean	Median	Minimum	Maximum
Entire Sample	15.56	10.00	0.00	90.00

Table 2.2: In your view, about what percentage of students who have not taken any formal information literacy training know a few of the essentials of Boolean searching such as the use of quotation marks, use of "or", "and" or the +/- plus signs to focus searches? Broken Out by Type of College

Type of College	Mean	Median	Minimum	Maximum
Community College	10.86	5.00	0.00	90.00
4-Year College	21.93	20.00	5.00	50.00
MA or PHD Granting College	15.44	10.00	1.00	50.00
Research University	21.00	2.00	1.00	60.00

Table 2.3: In your view, about what percentage of students who have not taken any formal information literacy training know a few of the essentials of Boolean searching such as the use of quotation marks, use of "or", "and" or the +/- plus signs to focus searches? Broken Out by Public or Private Status

Public or Private Status	Mean	Median	Minimum	Maximum
Public	14.57	10.00	0.00	90.00
Private	17.61	10.00	0.00	60.00

Table 2.4: In your view, about what percentage of students who have not taken any formal information literacy training know a few of the essentials of Boolean searching such as the use of quotation marks, use of "or", "and" or the +/- plus signs to focus searches? Broken Out by Total Student Enrollment

Total Student Enrollment	Mean	Median	Minimum	Maximum
Less than 2,500	10.65	10.00	0.00	25.00
2,500 to 5,000	14.06	10.00	0.00	90.00
More than 5,000	21.10	12.50	0.00	60.00

Table 2.5:   In your view, about what percentage of students who have not taken any formal information literacy training know a few of the essentials of Boolean searching such as the use of quotation marks, use of "or", "and" or the +/- plus signs to focus searches? Broken Out by Total Number of Instruction or Presentation Sessions given by the College's Librarians in the Past Year

Number of Instruction Sessions given by College	Mean	Median	Minimum	Maximum
Less than 100	8.53	8.00	0.00	25.00
100 to 200	18.00	15.00	0.00	50.00
More than 200	20.71	10.00	0.00	90.00

Table 2.6:   How would you rate the ability of your student body to assess the credibility of information from websites?

	Highly Proficient	Competent	Have a Basic Knowledge	Very Unskilled
Entire Sample	0.00%	18.33%	51.67%	30.00%

Table 2.7:   How would you rate the ability of your student body to assess the credibility of information from websites? Broken Out by Type of College

Type of College	Highly Proficient	Competent	Have a Basic Knowledge	Very Unskilled
Community College	0.00%	16.67%	29.17%	54.17%
4-Year College	0.00%	23.53%	64.71%	11.76%
MA or PHD Granting College	0.00%	12.50%	75.00%	12.50%
Research University	0.00%	33.33%	33.33%	33.33%

Table 2.8:   How would you rate the ability to assess the credibility of information from websites of your student body? Broken Out by Public or Private Status

Public or Private Status	Highly Proficient	Competent	Have a Basic Knowledge	Very Unskilled
Public	0.00%	15.00%	50.00%	35.00%
Private	0.00%	25.00%	55.00%	20.00%

Table 2.9:   How would you rate the ability of your student body to assess the credibility of information from websites? Broken Out by Total Student Enrollment

Total Student Enrollment	Highly Proficient	Competent	Have a Basic Knowledge	Very Unskilled
Less than 2,500	0.00%	16.67%	55.56%	27.78%
2,500 to 5,000	0.00%	14.29%	47.62%	38.10%
More than 5,000	0.00%	23.81%	52.38%	23.81%

Table 2.10:   How would you rate the ability of your student body to assess the credibility of information from websites? Broken Out by Total Number of Instruction or Presentation Sessions given by the College's Librarians in the Past Year

Number of Instruction Sessions given by College	Highly Proficient	Competent	Have a Basic Knowledge	Very Unskilled
Less than 100	0.00%	9.52%	57.14%	33.33%
100 to 200	0.00%	14.29%	61.90%	23.81%
More than 200	0.00%	33.33%	33.33%	33.33%

Table 2.11:   How would you rate your student body's knowledge of the basic concept of plagiarism and how to avoid it?

	Highly Proficient	Competent	Have a Basic Knowledge	Very Unskilled
Entire Sample	1.67%	20.00%	63.33%	15.00%

Table 2.12:   How would you rate your student body's knowledge of the basic concept of plagiarism and how to avoid it? Broken Out by Type of College

Type of College	Highly Proficient	Competent	Have a Basic Knowledge	Very Unskilled
Community College	0.00%	8.33%	62.50%	29.17%
4-Year College	0.00%	29.41%	64.71%	5.88%
MA or PHD Granting College	6.25%	25.00%	62.50%	6.25%
Research University	0.00%	33.33%	66.67%	0.00%

Table 2.13: How would you rate your student body's knowledge of the basic concept of plagiarism and how to avoid it? Broken Out by Public or Private Status

Public or Private Status	Highly Proficient	Competent	Have a Basic Knowledge	Very Unskilled
Public	0.00%	20.00%	60.00%	20.00%
Private	5.00%	20.00%	70.00%	5.00%

Table 2.14: How would you rate your student body's knowledge of the basic concept of plagiarism and how to avoid it? Broken Out by Total Student Enrollment

Total Student Enrollment	Highly Proficient	Competent	Have a Basic Knowledge	Very Unskilled
Less than 2,500	0.00%	33.33%	55.56%	11.11%
2,500 to 5,000	0.00%	19.05%	61.90%	19.05%
More than 5,000	4.76%	9.52%	71.43%	14.29%

Table 2.15: How would you rate your student body's knowledge of the basic concept of plagiarism and how to avoid it? Broken Out by Total Number of Instruction or Presentation Sessions given by the College's Librarians in the Past Year

Number of Instruction Sessions given by College	Highly Proficient	Competent	Have a Basic Knowledge	Very Unskilled
Less than 100	0.00%	33.33%	47.62%	19.05%
100 to 200	4.76%	19.05%	57.14%	19.05%
More than 200	0.00%	5.56%	88.89%	5.56%

Table 2.16: How would you rate the ability of your student body to use the online library catalogue?

	Highly Proficient	Competent	Have a Basic Knowledge	Very Unskilled
Entire Sample	0.00%	26.67%	51.67%	21.67%

Table 2.17: How would you rate the ability of your student body to use the online library catalogue? Broken Out by Type of College

Type of College	Highly Proficient	Competent	Have a Basic Knowledge	Very Unskilled
Community College	0.00%	20.83%	45.83%	33.33%
4-Year College	0.00%	35.29%	52.94%	11.76%
MA or PHD Granting College	0.00%	31.25%	56.25%	12.50%
Research University	0.00%	0.00%	66.67%	33.33%

Table 2.18: How would you rate the ability of your student body to use the online library catalogue? Broken Out by Public or Private Status

Public or Private Status	Highly Proficient	Competent	Have a Basic Knowledge	Very Unskilled
Public	0.00%	25.00%	50.00%	25.00%
Private	0.00%	30.00%	55.00%	15.00%

Table 2.19: How would you rate the ability of your student body to use the online library catalogue? Broken Out by Total Student Enrollment

Total Student Enrollment	Highly Proficient	Competent	Have a Basic Knowledge	Very Unskilled
Less than 2,500	0.00%	27.78%	44.44%	27.78%
2,500 to 5,000	0.00%	23.81%	61.90%	14.29%
More than 5,000	0.00%	28.57%	47.62%	23.81%

Table 2.20: How would you rate the ability of your student body to use the online library catalogue? Broken Out by Total Number of Instruction or Presentation Sessions given by the College's Librarians in the Past Year

Number of Instruction Sessions given by College	Highly Proficient	Competent	Have a Basic Knowledge	Very Unskilled
Less than 100	0.00%	33.33%	38.10%	28.57%
100 to 200	0.00%	14.29%	71.43%	14.29%
More than 200	0.00%	33.33%	44.44%	22.22%

Table 2.21:   How would you rate the ability of your student body to use search engines?

	Highly Proficient	Competent	Have a Basic Knowledge	Very Unskilled
Entire Sample	1.67%	41.67%	50.00%	6.67%

Table 2.22:   How would you rate the ability of your student body to use search engines? Broken Out by Type of College

Type of College	Highly Proficient	Competent	Have a Basic Knowledge	Very Unskilled
Community College	0.00%	37.50%	58.33%	4.17%
4-Year College	5.88%	47.06%	41.18%	5.88%
MA or PHD Granting College	0.00%	50.00%	43.75%	6.25%
Research University	0.00%	0.00%	66.67%	33.33%

Table 2.23:   How would you rate the ability of your student body to use search engines? Broken Out by Public or Private Status

Public or Private Status	Highly Proficient	Competent	Have a Basic Knowledge	Very Unskilled
Public	2.50%	35.00%	55.00%	7.50%
Private	0.00%	55.00%	40.00%	5.00%

Table 2.24:   How would you rate the ability of your student body to use search engines? Broken Out by Total Student Enrollment

Total Student Enrollment	Highly Proficient	Competent	Have a Basic Knowledge	Very Unskilled
Less than 2,500	0.00%	50.00%	44.44%	5.56%
2,500 to 5,000	0.00%	33.33%	61.90%	4.76%
More than 5,000	4.76%	42.86%	42.86%	9.52%

Table 2.25: How would you rate the ability of your student body to use search engines? Broken Out by Total Number of Instruction or Presentation Sessions given by the College's Librarians in the Past Year

Number of Instruction Sessions given by College	Highly Proficient	Competent	Have a Basic Knowledge	Very Unskilled
Less than 100	0.00%	33.33%	61.90%	4.76%
100 to 200	0.00%	42.86%	52.38%	4.76%
More than 200	5.56%	50.00%	33.33%	11.11%

Table 2.26: How would you rate the ability of your student body to use periodicals databases?

	Highly Proficient	Competent	Have a Basic Knowledge	Very Unskilled
Entire Sample	3.33%	10.00%	48.33%	38.33%

Table 2.27: How would you rate the ability of your student body to use periodicals databases? Broken Out by Type of College

Type of College	Highly Proficient	Competent	Have a Basic Knowledge	Very Unskilled
Community College	4.17%	8.33%	41.67%	45.83%
4-Year College	5.88%	5.88%	52.94%	35.29%
MA or PHD Granting College	0.00%	12.50%	56.25%	31.25%
Research University	0.00%	33.33%	33.33%	33.33%

Table 2.28: How would you rate the ability of your student body to use periodicals databases? Broken Out by Public or Private Status

Public or Private Status	Highly Proficient	Competent	Have a Basic Knowledge	Very Unskilled
Public	2.50%	10.00%	45.00%	42.50%
Private	5.00%	10.00%	55.00%	30.00%

Table 2.29: How would you rate the ability of your student body to use periodicals databases? Broken Out by Total Student Enrollment

Total Student Enrollment	Highly Proficient	Competent	Have a Basic Knowledge	Very Unskilled
Less than 2,500	11.11%	5.56%	38.89%	44.44%
2,500 to 5,000	0.00%	14.29%	52.38%	33.33%
More than 5,000	0.00%	9.52%	52.38%	38.10%

Table 2.30: How would you rate the ability of your student body to use periodicals databases? Broken Out by Total Number of Instruction or Presentation Sessions given by the College's Librarians in the Past Year

Number of Instruction Sessions given by College	Highly Proficient	Competent	Have a Basic Knowledge	Very Unskilled
Less than 100	4.76%	9.52%	47.62%	38.10%
100 to 200	0.00%	9.52%	47.62%	42.86%
More than 200	5.56%	11.11%	50.00%	33.33%

Table 2.31: How would you rate the ability of your student body to use e-book collections?

	Highly Proficient	Competent	Have a Basic Knowledge	Very Unskilled
Entire Sample	0.00%	8.47%	37.29%	54.24%

Table 2.32: How would you rate the ability of your student body to use e-book collections? Broken Out by Type of College

Type of College	Highly Proficient	Competent	Have a Basic Knowledge	Very Unskilled
Community College	0.00%	4.17%	37.50%	58.33%
4-Year College	0.00%	12.50%	37.50%	50.00%
MA or PHD Granting College	0.00%	12.50%	37.50%	50.00%
Research University	0.00%	0.00%	33.33%	66.67%

Table 2.33: How would you rate the ability of your student body to use e-book collections? Broken Out by Public or Private Status

Public or Private Status	Highly Proficient	Competent	Have a Basic Knowledge	Very Unskilled
Public	0.00%	5.00%	37.50%	57.50%
Private	0.00%	15.79%	36.84%	47.37%

Table 2.34: How would you rate the ability of your student body to use e-book collections? Broken Out by Total Student Enrollment

Total Student Enrollment	Highly Proficient	Competent	Have a Basic Knowledge	Very Unskilled
Less than 2,500	0.00%	11.76%	23.53%	64.71%
2,500 to 5,000	0.00%	9.52%	47.62%	42.86%
More than 5,000	0.00%	4.76%	38.10%	57.14%

Table 2.35: How would you rate the ability of your student body to use e-book collections? Broken Out by Total Number of Instruction or Presentation Sessions given by the College's Librarians in the Past Year

Number of Instruction Sessions given by College	Highly Proficient	Competent	Have a Basic Knowledge	Very Unskilled
Less than 100	0.00%	9.52%	38.10%	52.38%
100 to 200	0.00%	9.52%	33.33%	57.14%
More than 200	0.00%	5.88%	41.18%	52.94%

Table 2.36: How would you rate the ability of your student body to use major databases?

	Highly Proficient	Competent	Have a Basic Knowledge	Very Unskilled
Entire Sample	3.33%	21.67%	41.67%	33.33%

Table 2.37: How would you rate the ability of your student body to use major databases? Broken Out by Type of College

Type of College	Highly Proficient	Competent	Have a Basic Knowledge	Very Unskilled
Community College	4.17%	16.67%	33.33%	45.83%
4-Year College	5.88%	11.76%	58.82%	23.53%
MA or PHD Granting College	0.00%	31.25%	43.75%	25.00%
Research University	0.00%	66.67%	0.00%	33.33%

Table 2.38: How would you rate the ability of your student body to use major databases? Broken Out by Public or Private Status

Public or Private Status	Highly Proficient	Competent	Have a Basic Knowledge	Very Unskilled
Public	2.50%	22.50%	37.50%	37.50%
Private	5.00%	20.00%	50.00%	25.00%

Table 2.39: How would you rate the ability of your student body to use major databases? Broken Out by Total Student Enrollment

Total Student Enrollment	Highly Proficient	Competent	Have a Basic Knowledge	Very Unskilled
Less than 2,500	11.11%	16.67%	38.89%	33.33%
2,500 to 5,000	0.00%	14.29%	47.62%	38.10%
More than 5,000	0.00%	33.33%	38.10%	28.57%

Table 2.40: How would you rate the ability of your student body to use major databases? Broken Out by Total Number of Instruction or Presentation Sessions given by the College's Librarians in the Past Year

Number of Instruction Sessions given by College	Highly Proficient	Competent	Have a Basic Knowledge	Very Unskilled
Less than 100	4.76%	23.81%	38.10%	33.33%
100 to 200	0.00%	19.05%	47.62%	33.33%
More than 200	5.56%	22.22%	38.89%	33.33%

Table 2.41:   How would you rate the ability of your student body to use library special collections?

	Highly Proficient	Competent	Have a Basic Knowledge	Very Unskilled
Entire Sample	0.00%	1.72%	31.03%	67.24%

Table 2.42:   How would you rate the ability of your student body to use library special collections? Broken Out by Type of College

Type of College	Highly Proficient	Competent	Have a Basic Knowledge	Very Unskilled
Community College	0.00%	4.35%	30.43%	65.22%
4-Year College	0.00%	0.00%	43.75%	56.25%
MA or PHD Granting College	0.00%	0.00%	18.75%	81.25%
Research University	0.00%	0.00%	33.33%	66.67%

Table 2.43:   How would you rate the ability of your student body to use library special collections? Broken Out by Public or Private Status

Public or Private Status	Highly Proficient	Competent	Have a Basic Knowledge	Very Unskilled
Public	0.00%	2.56%	28.21%	69.23%
Private	0.00%	0.00%	36.84%	63.16%

Table 2.44:   How would you rate the ability of your student body to use library special collections? Broken Out by Total Student Enrollment

Total Student Enrollment	Highly Proficient	Competent	Have a Basic Knowledge	Very Unskilled
Less than 2,500	0.00%	0.00%	35.29%	64.71%
2,500 to 5,000	0.00%	0.00%	25.00%	75.00%
More than 5,000	0.00%	4.76%	33.33%	61.90%

Table 2.45:   How would you rate the ability of your student body to use library special collections? Broken Out by Total Number of Instruction or Presentation Sessions given by the College's Librarians in the Past Year

Number of Instruction Sessions given by College	Highly Proficient	Competent	Have a Basic Knowledge	Very Unskilled
Less than 100	0.00%	5.00%	35.00%	60.00%
100 to 200	0.00%	0.00%	25.00%	75.00%
More than 200	0.00%	0.00%	33.33%	66.67%

Chapter 3: Testing & Assessment

Table 3.1: Has the college ever administered a test to assess student skills in use of the college online catalogue?

	Yes	No
Entire Sample	25.00%	75.00%

Table 3.2: Has the college ever administered a test to assess student skills in use of the college online catalogue? Broken Out by Type of College

Type of College	Yes	No
Community College	25.00%	75.00%
4-Year College	11.76%	88.24%
MA or PHD Granting College	37.50%	62.50%
Research University	33.33%	66.67%

Table 3.3: Has the college ever administered a test to assess student skills in use of the college online catalogue? Broken Out by Public or Private Status

Public or Private Status	Yes	No
Public	27.50%	72.50%
Private	20.00%	80.00%

Table 3.4: Has the college ever administered a test to assess student skills in use of the college online catalogue? Broken Out by Total Student Enrollment

Total Student Enrollment	Yes	No
Less than 2,500	22.22%	77.78%
2,500 to 5,000	14.29%	85.71%
More than 5,000	38.10%	61.90%

Table 3.5: Has the college ever administered a test to assess student skills in use of the college online catalogue? Broken Out by Total Number of Instruction or Presentation Sessions given by the College's Librarians in the Past Year

Number of Instruction Sessions given by College Librarians	Yes	No
Less than 100	23.81%	76.19%
100 to 200	23.81%	76.19%
More than 200	27.78%	72.22%

Table 3.6:   Has the college ever administered a test to assess student skills in the use of search engines and general web navigability?

	Yes	No
Entire Sample	20.00%	80.00%

Table 3.7:   Has the college ever administered a test to assess student skills in the use of search engines and general web navigability? Broken Out by Type of College

Type of College	Yes	No
Community College	12.50%	87.50%
4-Year College	23.53%	76.47%
MA or PHD Granting College	25.00%	75.00%
Research University	33.33%	66.67%

Table 3.8:   Has the college ever administered a test to assess student skills in the use of search engines and general web navigability? Broken Out by Public or Private Status

Public or Private Status	Yes	No
Public	20.00%	80.00%
Private	20.00%	80.00%

Table 3.9:   Has the college ever administered a test to assess student skills in the use of search engines and general web navigability? Broken Out by Total Student Enrollment

Total Student Enrollment	Yes	No
Less than 2,500	16.67%	83.33%
2,500 to 5,000	0.00%	100.00%
More than 2,500	42.86%	57.14%

Table 3.10:   Has the college ever administered a test to assess student skills in the use of search engines and general web navigability? Broken Out by Total Number of Instruction or Presentation Sessions given by the College's Librarians in the Past Year

Number of Instruction Sessions given by College Librarians	Yes	No
Less than 100	9.52%	90.48%
100 to 200	23.81%	76.19%
More than 200	27.78%	72.22%

Table 3.11: Has the college ever administered a test to assess student skills in the use of Word, WordPerfect or other word processing software?

	Yes	No
Entire Sample	16.67%	83.33%

Table 3.12: Has the college ever administered a test to assess student skills in the use of Word, WordPerfect or other word processing software? Broken Out by Type of College

Type of College	Yes	No
Community College	16.67%	83.33%
4-Year College	17.65%	82.35%
MA or PHD Granting College	18.75%	81.25%
Research University	0.00%	100.00%

Table 3.13: Has the college ever administered a test to assess student skills in the use of Word, WordPerfect or other word processing software? Broken Out by Public or Private Status

Public or Private Status	Yes	No
Public	12.50%	87.50%
Private	25.00%	75.00%

Table 3.14: Has the college ever administered a test to assess student skills in the use of Word, WordPerfect or other word processing software? Broken Out by Total Student Enrollment

Total Student Enrollment	Yes	No
Less than 2,500	33.33%	66.67%
2,500 to 5,000	4.76%	95.24%
More than 5,000	14.29%	85.71%

Table 3.15: Has the college ever administered a test to assess student skills in the use of Word, WordPerfect or other word processing software? Broken Out by Total Number of Instruction or Presentation Sessions given by the College's Librarians in the Past Year

Number of Instruction Sessions given by College Librarians	Yes	No
Less than 100	28.57%	71.43%
100 to 200	9.52%	90.48%
More than 200	11.11%	88.89%

Table 3.16:   Has the college ever administered a test to assess student skills in the use of Excel or other spreadsheet software?

	Yes	No
Entire Sample	11.67%	88.33%

Table 3.17:   Has the college ever administered a test to assess student skills in the use of Excel or other spreadsheet software? Broken Out by Type of College

Type of College	Yes	No
Community College	12.50%	87.50%
4-Year College	5.88%	94.12%
MA or PHD Granting College	18.75%	81.25%
Research University	0.00%	100.00%

Table 3.18:   Has the college ever administered a test to assess student skills in the use of Excel or other spreadsheet software? Broken Out by Public or Private Status

Public or Private Status	Yes	No
Public	10.00%	90.00%
Private	15.00%	85.00%

Table 3.19:   Has the college ever administered a test to assess student skills in the use of Excel or other spreadsheet software? Broken Out by Total Student Enrollment

Total Student Enrollment	Yes	No
Less than 2,500	22.22%	77.78%
2,500 to 5,000	0.00%	100.00%
More than 5,000	14.29%	85.71%

Table 3.20:   Has the college ever administered a test to assess student skills in the use of Excel or other spreadsheet software? Broken Out by Total Number of Instruction or Presentation Sessions given by the College's Librarians in the Past Year

Number of Instruction Sessions given by College Librarians	Yes	No
Less than 100	14.29%	85.71%
100 to 200	9.52%	90.48%
More than 200	11.11%	88.89%

Table 3.21: Has the college ever administered a test to assess student skills in the use of Windows?

	Yes	No
Entire Sample	10.00%	90.00%

Table 3.22: Has the college ever administered a test to assess student skills in the use of Windows? Broken Out by Type of College

Type of College	Yes	No
Community College	16.67%	83.33%
4-Year College	5.88%	94.12%
MA or PHD Granting College	6.25%	93.75%
Research University	0.00%	100.00%

Table 3.23: Has the college ever administered a test to assess student skills in the use of Windows? Broken Out by Public or Private Status

Public or Private Status	Yes	No
Public	10.00%	90.00%
Private	10.00%	90.00%

Table 3.24: Has the college ever administered a test to assess student skills in the use of Windows? Broken Out by Total Student Enrollment

Total Student Enrollment	Yes	No
Less than 2,500	16.67%	83.33%
2,500 to 5,000	4.76%	95.24%
More than 5,000	9.52%	90.48%

Table 3.25: Has the college ever administered a test to assess student skills in the use of Windows? Broken Out by Total Number of Instruction or Presentation Sessions given by the College's Librarians in the Past Year

Number of Instruction Sessions given by College Librarians	Yes	No
Less than 100	14.29%	85.71%
100 to 200	9.52%	90.48%
More than 200	5.56%	94.44%

Table 3.26: Does the library administer an information literacy test of some kind to incoming freshmen or transfers?

	Yes	No
Entire Sample	24.07%	75.93%

Table 3.27:   Does the library administer an information literacy test of some kind to incoming freshmen or transfers? Broken Out by Type of College

Type of College	Yes	No
Community College	13.04%	86.96%
4-Year College	21.43%	78.57%
MA or PHD Granting College	42.86%	57.15%
Research University	33.33%	66.67%

Table 3.28:   Does the library administer an information literacy test of some kind to incoming freshmen or transfers? Broken Out by Public or Private Status

Public or Private Status	Yes	No
Public	25.71%	74.29%
Private	21.05%	78.95%

Table 3.29:   Does the library administer an information literacy test of some kind to incoming freshmen or transfers? Broken Out by Total Student Enrollment

Total Student Enrollment	Yes	No
Less than 2,500	17.65%	82.35%
2,500 to 5,000	16.67%	83.33%
More than 5,000	36.84%	63.16%

Table 3.30:   Does the library administer an information literacy test of some kind to incoming freshmen or transfers? Broken Out by Total Number of Instruction or Presentation Sessions given by the College's Librarians in the Past Year

Number of Instruction Sessions given by College Librarians	Yes	No
Less than 100	10.53%	89.47%
100 to 200	36.84%	63.16%
More than 200	25.00%	75.00%

Table 3.31:   Does the library administer an information literacy test to incoming freshmen or transfers for capacity to use periodicals databases?

	Yes	No
Entire Sample	20.37%	79.63%

Table 3.32:   Does the library administer an information literacy test to incoming freshmen or transfers for capacity to use periodicals databases? Broken Out by Type of College

Type of College	Yes	No
Community College	13.04%	86.96%
4-Year College	14.29%	85.71%
MA or PHD Granting College	35.71%	64.29%
Research University	33.33%	66.67%

Table 3.33:   Does the library administer an information literacy test to incoming freshmen or transfers for capacity to use periodicals databases? Broken Out by Public or Private Status

Public or Private Status	Yes	No
Public	22.86%	77.14%
Private	15.79%	84.21%

Table 3.34:   Does the library administer an information literacy test to incoming freshmen or transfers for capacity to use periodicals databases? Broken Out by Total Student Enrollment

Total Student Enrollment	Yes	No
Less than 2,500	17.65%	82.35%
2,500 to 5,000	5.56%	94.44%
More than 5,000	36.84%	63.16%

Table 3.35:   Does the library administer an information literacy test to incoming freshmen or transfers for capacity to use periodicals databases? Broken Out by Total Number of Instruction or Presentation Sessions given by the College's Librarians in the Past Year

Number of Instruction Sessions given by College Librarians	Yes	No
Less than 100	10.53%	89.47%
100 to 200	31.58%	68.42%
More than 200	18.75%	81.25%

Table 3.36:   Does the library administer an information literacy test to incoming freshmen or transfers for capacity to use the online library catalogue?

	Yes	No
Entire Sample	20.37%	79.63%

Table 3.37: Does the library administer an information literacy test to incoming freshmen or transfers for capacity to use the online library catalogue? Broken Out by Type of College

Type of College	Yes	No
Community College	13.04%	86.96%
4-Year College	14.29%	85.71%
MA or PHD Granting College	35.71%	64.29%
Research University	33.33%	66.67%

Table 3.38: Does the library administer an information literacy test to incoming freshmen or transfers for capacity to use the online library catalogue? Broken Out by Public or Private Status

Public or Private Status	Yes	No
Public	22.86%	77.14%
Private	15.79%	84.21%

Table 3.39: Does the library administer an information literacy test to incoming freshmen or transfers for capacity to use the online library catalogue? Broken Out by Total Student Enrollment

Total Student Enrollment	Yes	No
Less than 2,500	17.65%	82.35%
2,500 to 5,000	5.56%	94.44%
More than 5,000	36.84%	63.16%

Table 3.40: Does the library administer an information literacy test to incoming freshmen or transfers for capacity to use the online library catalogue? Broken Out by Total Number of Instruction or Presentation Sessions given by the College's Librarians in the Past Year

Number of Instruction Sessions given by College Librarians	Yes	No
Less than 100	10.53%	89.47%
100 to 200	31.58%	68.42%
More than 200	18.75%	81.25%

Table 3.41: Does the library administer an information literacy test to incoming freshmen or transfers for capabilities with search methodology?

	Yes	No
Entire Sample	18.52%	81.48%

Table 3.42:   Does the library administer an information literacy test to incoming freshmen or transfers for capabilities with search methodology? Broken Out by Type of College

Type of College	Yes	No
Community College	4.35%	95.65%
4-Year College	21.43%	78.57%
MA or PHD Granting College	35.71%	64.29%
Research University	33.33%	66.67%

Table 3.43:   Does the library administer an information literacy test to incoming freshmen or transfers for capabilities with search methodology? Broken Out by Public or Private Status

Public or Private Status	Yes	No
Public	17.14%	82.86%
Private	21.05%	78.95%

Table 3.44:   Does the library administer an information literacy test to incoming freshmen or transfers for capabilities with search methodology? Broken Out by Total Student Enrollment

Total Student Enrollment	Yes	No
Less than 2,500	17.65%	82.35%
2,500 to 5,000	5.56%	94.44%
More than 5,000	31.58%	68.42%

Table 3.45:   Does the library administer an information literacy test to incoming freshmen or transfers for capabilities with search methodology? Broken Out by Total Number of Instruction or Presentation Sessions given by the College's Librarians in the Past Year

Number of Instruction Sessions given by College Librarians	Yes	No
Less than 100	10.53%	89.47%
100 to 200	31.58%	68.42%
More than 200	12.50%	87.50%

Table 3.46:   Does the library administer an information literacy test to incoming freshmen or transfers for understanding of plagiarism?

	Yes	No
Entire Sample	12.96%	87.04%

Table 3.47: Does the library administer an information literacy test to incoming freshmen or transfers for understanding of plagiarism? Broken Out by Type of College

Type of College	Yes	No
Community College	4.35%	95.65%
4-Year College	14.29%	85.71%
MA or PHD Granting College	28.57%	71.43%
Research University	0.00%	100.00%

Table 3.48: Does the library administer an information literacy test to incoming freshmen or transfers for understanding of plagiarism? Broken Out by Public or Private Status

Public or Private Status	Yes	No
Public	11.43%	88.57%
Private	15.79%	84.21%

Table 3.49: Does the library administer an information literacy test to incoming freshmen or transfers for understanding of plagiarism? Broken Out by Total Student Enrollment

Total Student Enrollment	Yes	No
Less than 2,500	17.65%	82.35%
2,500 to 5,000	0.00%	100.00%
More than 5,000	21.05%	78.95%

Table 3.50: Does the library administer an information literacy test to incoming freshmen or transfers for understanding of plagiarism? Broken Out by Total Number of Instruction or Presentation Sessions given by the College's Librarians in the Past Year

Number of Instruction Sessions given by College Librarians	Yes	No
Less than 100	10.53%	89.47%
100 to 200	15.79%	84.21%
More than 200	12.50%	87.50%

Table 3.51: Does the library administer an information literacy test to incoming freshmen or transfers for capacity to use e-book collections?

	Yes	No
Entire Sample	0.00%	100.00%

Table 3.52:   Is any form of information or computer literacy test required for graduation?

	Yes	No	No, but we will probably adopt this soon
Entire Sample	15.00%	71.67%	13.33%

Table 3.53:   Is any form of information or computer literacy test required for graduation? Broken Out by Type of College

Type of College	Yes	No	No, but we will probably adopt this soon
Community College	12.50%	70.83%	16.67%
4-Year College	11.76%	76.47%	11.76%
MA or PHD Granting College	18.75%	75.00%	6.25%
Research University	33.33%	33.33%	33.33%

Table 3.54:   Is any form of information or computer literacy test required for graduation? Broken Out by Public or Private Status

Public or Private Status	Yes	No	No, but we will probably adopt this soon
Public	15.00%	75.00%	10.00%
Private	15.00%	65.00%	20.00%

Table 3.55:   Is any form of information or computer literacy test required for graduation? Broken Out by Total Student Enrollment

Total Student Enrollment	Yes	No	No, but we will probably adopt this soon
Less than 2,500	16.67%	61.11%	22.22%
2,500 to 5,000	4.76%	85.71%	9.52%
More than 5,000	23.81%	66.67%	9.52%

Table 3.56:   Is any form of information or computer literacy test required for graduation? Broken Out by Total Number of Instruction or Presentation Sessions given by the College's Librarians in the Past Year

Number of Instruction Sessions given by College Librarians	Yes	No	No, but we will probably adopt this soon
Less than 100	14.29%	61.90%	23.81%
100 to 200	23.81%	71.43%	4.76%
More than 200	5.56%	83.33%	11.11%

Table 3.57: Does the library use student evaluation forms to assess the performance of information literacy or other library science instructors?

	Yes	No
Entire Sample	61.67%	38.33%

Table 3.58: Does the library use student evaluation forms to assess the performance of information literacy or other library science instructors? Broken Out by Type of College

Type of College	Yes	No
Community College	62.50%	37.50%
4-Year College	64.71%	35.29%
MA or PHD Granting College	62.50%	37.50%
Research University	33.33%	66.67%

Table 3.59: Does the library use student evaluation forms to assess the performance of information literacy or other library science instructors? Broken Out by Public or Private Status

Public or Private Status	Yes	No
Public	60.00%	40.00%
Private	65.00%	35.00%

Table 3.60: Does the library use student evaluation forms to assess the performance of information literacy or other library science instructors? Broken Out by Total Student Enrollment

Total Student Enrollment	Yes	No
Less than 2,500	66.67%	33.33%
2,500 to 5,000	52.38%	47.62%
More than 5,000	66.67%	33.33%

Table 3.61: Does the library use student evaluation forms to assess the performance of information literacy or other library science instructors? Broken Out by Total Number of Instruction or Presentation Sessions given by the College's Librarians in the Past Year

Number of Instruction Sessions given by College Librarians	Yes	No
Less than 100	66.67%	33.33%
100 to 200	57.14%	42.86%
More than 200	61.11%	38.89%

Table 3.62:   Does the library videotape or record instruction sessions for later review?

	Yes	No
Entire Sample	3.33%	96.67%

Table 3.63:   Does the library videotape or record instruction sessions for later review? Broken Out by Type of College

Type of College	Yes	No
Community College	4.17%	95.83%
4-Year College	0.00%	100.00%
MA or PHD Granting College	6.25%	93.75%
Research University	0.00%	100.00%

Table 3.64:   Does the library videotape or record instruction sessions for later review? Broken Out by Public or Private Status

Public or Private Status	Yes	No
Public	5.00%	95.00%
Private	0.00%	100.00%

Table 3.65:   Does the library videotape or record instruction sessions for later review? Broken Out by Total Student Enrollment

Total Student Enrollment	Yes	No
Less than 2,500	0.00%	100.00%
2,500 to 5,000	9.52%	90.48%
More than 5,000	0.00%	100.00%

Table 3.66:   Does the library videotape or record instruction sessions for later review? Broken Out by Total Number of Instruction or Presentation Sessions given by the College's Librarians in the Past Year

Number of Instruction Sessions given by College Librarians	Yes	No
Less than 100	0.00%	100.00%
100 to 200	4.76%	95.24%
More than 200	5.56%	94.44%

Table 3.67:   Do senior librarians sit in on and evaluate library instruction classes?

	Yes	No
Entire Sample	10.00%	90.00%

Table 3.68: Do senior librarians sit in on and evaluate library instruction classes? Broken Out by Type of College

Type of College	Yes	No
Community College	4.17%	95.83%
4-Year College	17.65%	82.35%
MA or PHD Granting College	12.50%	87.50%
Research University	0.00%	100.00%

Table 3.69: Do senior librarians sit in on and evaluate library instruction classes? Broken Out by Public or Private Status

Public or Private Status	Yes	No
Public	12.50%	87.50%
Private	5.00%	95.00%

Table 3.70: Do senior librarians sit in on and evaluate library instruction classes? Broken Out by Total Student Enrollment

Total Student Enrollment	Yes	No
Less than 2,500	0.00%	100.00%
2,500 to 5,000	19.05%	80.95%
More than 5,000	9.52%	90.48%

Table 3.71: Do senior librarians sit in on and evaluate library instruction classes? Broken Out by Total Number of Instruction or Presentation Sessions given by the College's Librarians in the Past Year

Number of Instruction Sessions given by College Librarians	Yes	No
Less than 100	0.00%	100.00%
100 to 200	19.05%	80.95%
More than 200	11.11%	88.89%

Table 3.72: Does the library use student standardized test results to assess the performance of information literacy or other library science instructors?

	Yes	No
Entire Sample	18.33%	81.67%

Table 3.73:   Does the library use student standardized test results to assess the performance of information literacy or other library science instructors? Broken Out by Type of College

Type of College	Yes	No
Community College	16.67%	83.33%
4-Year College	29.41%	70.59%
MA or PHD Granting College	12.50%	87.50%
Research University	0.00%	100.00%

Table 3.74:   Does the library use student standardized test results to assess the performance of information literacy or other library science instructors? Broken Out by Public or Private Status

Public or Private Status	Yes	No
Public	17.50%	82.50%
Private	20.00%	80.00%

Table 3.75:   Does the library use student standardized test results to assess the performance of information literacy or other library science instructors? Broken Out by Total Student Enrollment

Total Student Enrollment	Yes	No
Less than 2,500	27.78%	72.22%
2,500 to 5,000	9.52%	90.48%
More than 5,000	19.05%	80.95%

Table 3.76:   Does the library use student standardized test results to assess the performance of information literacy or other library science instructors? Broken Out by Total Number of Instruction or Presentation Sessions given by the College's Librarians in the Past Year

Number of Instruction Sessions given by College Librarians	Yes	No
Less than 100	23.81%	76.19%
100 to 200	23.81%	76.19%
More than 200	5.56%	94.44%

Table 3.77:   In the past year did the library administer to college faculty a librarian education services evaluation form to assess satisfaction with library assistance to faculty?

	Yes	No
Entire Sample	31.67%	68.33%

Table 3.78: In the past year did the library administer to college faculty a librarian education services evaluation form to assess satisfaction with library assistance to faculty? Broken Out by Type of College

Type of College	Yes	No
Community College	33.33%	66.67%
4-Year College	29.41%	70.59%
MA or PHD Granting College	31.25%	68.75%
Research University	33.33%	66.67%

Table 3.79: In the past year did the library administer to college faculty a librarian education services evaluation form to assess satisfaction with library assistance to faculty? Broken Out by Public or Private Status

Public or Private Status	Yes	No
Public	35.00%	65.00%
Private	25.00%	75.00%

Table 3.80: In the past year did the library administer to college faculty a librarian education services evaluation form to assess satisfaction with library assistance to faculty? Broken Out by Total Student Enrollment

Total Student Enrollment	Yes	No
Less than 2,500	33.33%	66.67%
2,500 to 5,000	23.81%	76.19%
More than 5,000	38.10%	61.90%

Table 3.81: In the past year did the library administer to college faculty a librarian education services evaluation form to assess satisfaction with library assistance to faculty? Broken Out by Total Number of Instruction or Presentation Sessions given by the College's Librarians in the Past Year

Number of Instruction Sessions given by College Librarians	Yes	No
Less than 100	28.57%	71.43%
100 to 200	38.10%	61.90%
More than 200	27.78%	72.22%

Table 3.82: If the library has administered a library education services evaluation form to faculty in the past three years, how many did it distribute?

	Mean	Median	Minimum	Maximum
Entire Sample	464.44	59.00	9.00	6000.00

Table 3.83: If the library has administered a library education services evaluation form to faculty in the past three years, how many did it distribute? Broken Out by Public or Private Status

Public or Private Status	Mean	Median	Minimum	Maximum
Public	114.55	63.00	9.00	500.00
Private	1234.20	55.00	12.00	6000.00

Table 3.84: If the library has administered a library education services evaluation form to faculty in the past three years, how many did it distribute? Broken Out by Total Student Enrollment

Total Student Enrollment	Mean	Median	Minimum	Maximum
Less than 2,500	35.50	30.00	12.00	77.00
2,500 to 5,000	43.75	43.00	9.00	80.00
More than 5,000	1173.83	205.00	63.00	6000.00

Table 3.85: If the library has administered a library education services evaluation form to faculty in the past three years, how many did it distribute? Broken Out by Total Number of Instruction or Presentation Sessions given by the College's Librarians in the Past Year

Number of Instruction Sessions given by College Librarians	Mean	Median	Minimum	Maximum
Less than 100	42.75	35.00	24.00	77.00
100 to 200	132.29	70.00	9.00	500.00
More than 200	1266.80	63.00	30.00	6000.00

Table 3.86: If the library has administered a library education services evaluation form to faculty in the past three years, how many did it get back?

	Mean	Median	Minimum	Maximum
Entire Sample	109.65	38.00	2.00	915.00

Table 3.87: If the library has administered a library education services evaluation form to faculty in the past three years, how many did it get back? Broken Out by Public or Private Status

Public or Private Status	Mean	Median	Minimum	Maximum
Public	71.75	37.00	2.00	247.00
Private	200.60	38.00	4.00	915.00

Table 3.88:   If the library has administered a library education services evaluation form to faculty in the past three years, how many did it get back? Broken Out by Total Student Enrollment

Total Student Enrollment	Mean	Median	Minimum	Maximum
Less than 2,500	19.00	7.00	4.00	70.00
2,500 to 5,000	23.00	25.00	2.00	40.00
More than 5,000	236.86	160.00	35.00	915.00

Table 3.89:   If the library has administered a library education services evaluation form to faculty in the past three years, how many did it get back? Broken Out by Total Number of Instruction or Presentation Sessions given by the College's Librarians in the Past Year

Number of Instruction Sessions given by College Librarians	Mean	Median	Minimum	Maximum
Less than 100	25.50	14.00	4.00	70.00
100 to 200	54.71	38.00	2.00	174.00
More than 200	229.83	99.50	6.00	915.00

*Not enough information to calculate the number of library education services evaluation forms administered to faculty broken out by type of college

Chapter 4: Student Orientation

Table 4.1: Does the library make presentations or give brief classes to new students during the new student orientation?

	Yes	No
Entire Sample	56.67%	43.33%

Table 4.2: Does the library make presentations or give brief classes to new students during the new student orientation? Broken Out by Type of College

Type of College	Yes	No
Community College	45.83%	54.17%
4-Year College	76.47%	23.53%
MA or PHD Granting College	56.25%	43.75%
Research University	33.33%	66.67%

Table 4.3: Does the library make presentations or give brief classes to new students during the new student orientation? Broken Out by Public or Private Status

Public or Private Status	Yes	No
Public	52.50%	47.50%
Private	65.00%	35.00%

Table 4.4: Does the library make presentations or give brief classes to new students during the new student orientation? Broken Out by Total Student Enrollment

Total Student Enrollment	Yes	No
Less than 2,500	61.11%	38.89%
2,500 to 5,000	57.14%	42.86%
More than 5,000	52.38%	47.62%

Table 4.5: Does the library make presentations or give brief classes to new students during the new student orientation? Broken Out by Total Number of Instruction or Presentation Sessions given by the College's Librarians in the Past Year

Number of Instruction Sessions given by College Librarians	Yes	No
Less than 100	61.90%	38.10%
100 to 200	52.38%	47.62%
More than 200	55.56%	44.44%

Table 4.6: If the library makes presentations or gives classes to incoming students during their orientation, what is the average amount of time (in hours) that students spend in these library sessions during orientation?

	Mean	Median	Minimum	Maximum
Entire Sample	0.66	0.75	0.15	1.50

Table 4.7: If the library makes presentations or gives classes to incoming students during their orientation, what is the average amount of time (in hours) that students spend in these library sessions during orientation? Broken Out by Type of College

Type of College	Mean	Median	Minimum	Maximum
Community College	0.46	0.33	0.15	0.85
4-Year College	0.76	0.85	0.25	1.50
MA or PHD Granting College	0.84	1.00	0.25	1.00
Research University	0.20	0.20	0.20	0.20

Table 4.8: If the library makes presentations or gives classes to incoming students during their orientation, what is the average amount of time (in hours) that students spend in these library sessions during orientation? Broken Out by Public or Private Status

Public or Private Status	Mean	Median	Minimum	Maximum
Public	0.61	0.75	0.15	1.00
Private	0.73	0.88	0.17	1.50

Table 4.9: If the library makes presentations or gives classes to incoming students during their orientation, what is the average amount of time (in hours) that students spend in these library sessions during orientation? Broken Out by Total Student Enrollment

Total Student Enrollment	Mean	Median	Minimum	Maximum
Less than 2,500	0.61	0.50	0.33	1.00
2,500 to 5,000	0.58	0.75	0.15	1.00
More than 5,000	0.81	1.00	0.20	1.50

Table 4.10: If the library makes presentations or gives classes to incoming students during their orientation, what is the average amount of time (in hours) that students spend in these library sessions during orientation? Broken Out by Total Number of Instruction or Presentation Sessions given by the College's Librarians in the Past Year

Number of Instruction Sessions given by College Librarians	Mean	Median	Minimum	Maximum
Less than 100	0.59	0.50	0.17	1.00
100 to 200	0.86	1.00	0.25	1.50
More than 200	0.50	0.33	0.15	1.00

Table 4.11: Does the library participate in any kind of orientation or information literacy training class or period designed especially for distance learning students?

	Yes	No	Do not offer distance learning
Entire Sample	41.67%	55.00%	3.33%

Table 4.12: Does the library participate in any kind of orientation or information literacy training class or period designed especially for distance learning students? Broken Out by Type of College

Type of College	Yes	No	Do not offer distance learning
Community College	37.50%	62.50%	0.00%
4-Year College	35.29%	58.82%	5.88%
MA or PHD Granting College	56.25%	43.75%	0.00%
Research University	33.33%	33.33%	33.33%

Table 4.13: Does the library participate in any kind of orientation or information literacy training class or period designed especially for distance learning students? Broken Out by Public or Private Status

Public or Private Status	Yes	No	Do not offer distance learning
Public	37.50%	62.50%	0.00%
Private	50.00%	40.00%	10.00%

Table 4.14: Does the library participate in any kind of orientation or information literacy training class or period designed especially for distance learning students? Broken Out by Total Student Enrollment

Total Student Enrollment	Yes	No	Do not offer distance learning
Less than 2,500	33.33%	61.11%	5.56%
2,500 to 5,000	47.62%	52.38%	0.00%
More than 5,000	42.86%	52.38%	4.76%

Table 4.15: Does the library participate in any kind of orientation or information literacy training class or period designed especially for distance learning students? Broken Out by Total Number of Instruction or Presentation Sessions given by the College's Librarians in the Past Year

Number of Instruction Sessions given by College Librarians	Yes	No	Do not offer distance learning
Less than 100	42.86%	57.14%	0.00%
100 to 200	33.33%	61.90%	4.76%
More than 200	50.00%	44.44%	5.56%

Chapter 5: Requirements

Table 5.1: Does the college have a formal information literacy requirement for graduation?

	Yes	No
Entire Sample	28.33%	71.67%

Table 5.2: Does the college have a formal information literacy requirement for graduation? Broken Out by Type of College

Type of College	Yes	No
Community College	29.17%	70.83%
4-Year College	29.41%	70.59%
MA or PHD Granting College	25.00%	75.00%
Research University	33.33%	66.67%

Table 5.3: Does the college have a formal information literacy requirement for graduation? Broken Out by Public or Private Status

Public or Private Status	Yes	No
Public	25.00%	75.00%
Private	35.00%	65.00%

Table 5.4: Does the college have a formal information literacy requirement for graduation? Broken Out by Total Student Enrollment

Total Student Enrollment	Yes	No
Less than 2,500	38.89%	61.11%
2.500 to 5,000	14.29%	85.71%
More than 5,000	33.33%	66.67%

Table 5.5: Does the college have a formal information literacy requirement for graduation? Broken Out by Total Number of Instruction or Presentation Sessions given by the College's Librarians in the Past Year

Number of Instruction Sessions given by College Librarians	Yes	No
Less than 100	23.81%	76.19%
100 to 200	33.33%	66.67%
More than 200	27.78%	72.22%

Table 5.6:   Does the college require a one or two credit information
literacy course for graduation?

	Yes	No
Entire Sample	5.00%	95.00%

Table 5.7:   Does the college require a one or two credit information
literacy course for graduation? Broken Out by Type of College

Type of College	Yes	No
Community College	0.00%	100.00%
4-Year College	5.88%	94.12%
MA or PHD Granting College	12.50%	87.50%
Research University	0.00%	100.00%

Table 5.8:   Does the college require a one or two credit information
literacy course for graduation? Broken Out by Public or Private Status

Public or Private Status	Yes	No
Public	7.50%	92.50%
Private	0.00%	100.00%

Table 5.9:   Does the college require a one or two credit information
literacy course for graduation? Broken Out by Total Student Enrollment

Total Student Enrollment	Yes	No
Less than 2,500	5.56%	94.44%
2.500 to 5,000	0.00%	100.00%
More than 5,000	9.52%	90.48%

Table 5.10:   Does the college require a one or two credit information
literacy course for graduation? Broken Out by Total Number of Instruction or
Presentation Sessions given by the College's Librarians in the Past Year

Number of Instruction Sessions given by College Librarians	Yes	No
Less than 100	0.00%	100.00%
100 to 200	9.52%	90.48%
More than 200	5.56%	94.44%

Table 5.11: **Does the college require a three credit (or more) information literacy course for graduation?**

	Yes	No
Entire Sample	0.00%	100.00%

Table 5.12: **Does the college require information literacy training integrated into basic writing or composition courses for graduation?**

	Yes	No
Entire Sample	13.33%	86.67%

Table 5.13: **Does the college require information literacy training integrated into basic writing or composition courses for graduation? Broken Out by Type of College**

Type of College	Yes	No
Community College	20.83%	79.17%
4-Year College	5.88%	94.12%
MA or PHD Granting College	12.50%	87.50%
Research University	0.00%	100.00%

Table 5.14: **Does the college require information literacy training integrated into basic writing or composition courses for graduation? Broken Out by Public or Private Status**

Public or Private Status	Yes	No
Public	12.50%	87.50%
Private	15.00%	85.00%

Table 5.15: **Does the college require information literacy training integrated into basic writing or composition courses for graduation? Broken Out by Total Student Enrollment**

Total Student Enrollment	Yes	No
Less than 2,500	16.67%	83.33%
2.500 to 5,000	4.76%	95.24%
More than 5,000	19.05%	80.95%

Table 5.16:   Does the college require information literacy training integrated into basic writing or composition courses for graduation? Broken Out by Total Number of Instruction or Presentation Sessions given by the College's Librarians in the Past Year

Number of Instruction Sessions given by College Librarians	Yes	No
Less than 100	9.52%	90.48%
100 to 200	14.29%	85.71%
More than 200	16.67%	83.33%

Table 5.17:   Does the college require information literacy training integrated into basic courses in areas other than writing or composition for graduation?

	Yes	No
Entire Sample	16.67%	83.33%

Table 5.18:   Does the college require information literacy training integrated into basic courses in areas other than writing or composition for graduation? Broken Out by Type of College

Type of College	Yes	No
Community College	12.50%	87.50%
4-Year College	29.41%	70.59%
MA or PHD Granting College	12.50%	87.50%
Research University	0.00%	100.00%

Table 5.19:   Does the college require information literacy training integrated into basic courses in areas other than writing or composition for graduation? Broken Out by Public or Private Status

Public or Private Status	Yes	No
Public	7.50%	92.50%
Private	35.00%	65.00%

Table 5.20:   Does the college require information literacy training integrated into basic courses in areas other than writing or composition for graduation? Broken Out by Total Student Enrollment

Total Student Enrollment	Yes	No
Less than 2,500	38.89%	61.11%
2.500 to 5,000	4.76%	95.24%
More than 5,000	9.52%	90.48%

Table 5.21: Does the college require information literacy training integrated into basic courses in areas other than writing or composition for graduation? Broken Out by Total Number of Instruction or Presentation Sessions given by the College's Librarians in the Past Year

Number of Instruction Sessions given by College Librarians	Yes	No
Less than 100	23.81%	76.19%
100 to 200	19.05%	80.95%
More than 200	5.56%	94.44%

Table 5.22: If your college does not have a formal information literacy course requirement, how likely is it than it will adopt one within the next three years?

	Unlikely	It's possible but not likely	We have something in the pipeline and approval is likely	We already have approval and will implement very soon
Entire Sample	28.57%	59.18%	8.16%	4.08%

Table 5.23: If your college does not have a formal information literacy course requirement, how likely is it than it will adopt one within the next three years? Broken Out by Type of College

Type of College	Unlikely	It's possible but not likely	We have something in the pipeline and approval is likely	We already have approval and will implement very soon
Community College	45.00%	50.00%	5.00%	0.00%
4-Year College	23.08%	69.23%	7.69%	0.00%
MA or PHD Granting College	15.38%	61.54%	15.38%	7.69%
Research University	0.00%	66.67%	0.00%	33.33%

Table 5.24: If your college does not have a formal information literacy course requirement, how likely is it than it will adopt one within the next three years? Broken Out by Public or Private Status

Public or Private Status	Unlikely	It's possible but not likely	We have something in the pipeline and approval is likely	We already have approval and will implement very soon
Public	30.30%	57.58%	9.09%	3.03%
Private	25.00%	62.50%	6.25%	6.25%

Table 5.25: If your college does not have a formal information literacy course requirement, how likely is it than it will adopt one within the next three years? Broken Out by Total Student Enrollment

Total Student Enrollment	Unlikely	It's possible but not likely	We have something in the pipeline and approval is likely	We already have approval and will implement very soon
Less than 2,500	38.46%	53.85%	7.69%	0.00%
2.500 to 5,000	26.32%	63.16%	10.53%	0.00%
More than 5,000	23.53%	58.82%	5.88%	11.76%

Table 5.26: If your college does not have a formal information literacy course requirement, how likely is it than it will adopt one within the next three years? Broken Out by Total Number of Instruction or Presentation Sessions given by the College's Librarians in the Past Year

Number of Instruction Sessions given by College Librarians	Unlikely	It's possible but not likely	We have something in the pipeline and approval is likely	We already have approval and will implement very soon
Less than 100	55.56%	38.89%	5.56%	0.00%
100 to 200	17.65%	64.71%	5.88%	11.76%
More than 200	7.14%	78.57%	14.29%	0.00%

Table 5.27: Does the college offer any online or distance learning information literacy courses?

	Yes	No
Entire Sample	26.67%	73.33%

Table 5.28: Does the college offer any online or distance learning information literacy courses? Broken Out by Type of College

Type of College	Yes	No
Community College	29.17%	70.83%
4-Year College	11.76%	88.24%
MA or PHD Granting College	37.50%	62.50%
Research University	33.33%	66.67%

Table 5.29: Does the college offer any online or distance learning information literacy courses? Broken Out by Public or Private Status

Public or Private Status	Yes	No
Public	32.50%	67.50%
Private	15.00%	85.00%

Table 5.30: Does the college offer any online or distance learning information literacy courses? Broken Out by Total Student Enrollment

Total Student Enrollment	Yes	No
Less than 2,500	22.22%	77.78%
2,500 to 5,000	19.05%	80.95%
More than 5,000	38.10%	61.90%

Table 5.31: Does the college offer any online or distance learning information literacy courses? Broken Out by Total Number of Instruction or Presentation Sessions given by the College's Librarians in the Past Year

Number of Instruction Sessions given by College Librarians	Yes	No
Less than 100	23.81%	76.19%
100 to 200	23.81%	76.19%
More than 200	33.33%	66.67%

Chapter 6: Power and Influence

Table 6.1: Do any librarians currently serve on the college curriculum committee or its equivalent?

	Yes	No
Entire Sample	71.67%	28.33%

Table 6.2: Do any librarians currently serve on the college curriculum committee or its equivalent? Broken Out by Type of College

Type of College	Yes	No
Community College	70.83%	29.17%
4-Year College	70.59%	29.41%
MA or PHD Granting College	75.00%	25.00%
Research University	66.67%	33.33%

Table 6.3: Do any librarians currently serve on the college curriculum committee or its equivalent? Broken Out by Public or Private Status

Public or Private Status	Yes	No
Public	75.00%	25.00%
Private	65.00%	35.00%

Table 6.4: Do any librarians currently serve on the college curriculum committee or its equivalent? Broken Out by Total Student Enrollment

Total Student Enrollment	Yes	No
Less than 2,500	66.67%	33.33%
2,500 to 5,000	80.95%	19.05%
More than 5,000	66.67%	33.33%

Table 6.5: Do any librarians currently serve on the college curriculum committee or its equivalent? Broken Out by Total Number of Instruction or Presentation Sessions given by the College's Librarians in the Past Year

Number of Instruction Sessions given by College Librarians	Yes	No
Less than 100	66.67%	33.33%
100 to 200	80.95%	19.05%
More than 200	66.67%	33.33%

Table 6.6: Does the library offer any information literacy courses that are cross listed with other departments, such as computer science, psychology, history, biology, etc, or schools, such as a medical or law school?

	Yes	No
Entire Sample	15.00%	85.00%

Table 6.7: Does the library offer any information literacy courses that are cross listed with other departments, such as computer science, psychology, history, biology, etc, or schools, such as a medical or law school? Broken Out by Type of College

Type of College	Yes	No
Community College	4.17%	95.83%
4-Year College	17.65%	82.35%
MA or PHD Granting College	18.75%	81.25%
Research University	66.67%	33.33%

Table 6.8: Does the library offer any information literacy courses that are cross listed with other departments, such as computer science, psychology, history, biology, etc, or schools, such as a medical or law school? Broken Out by Public or Private Status

Public or Private Status	Yes	No
Public	7.50%	92.50%
Private	30.00%	70.00%

Table 6.9: Does the library offer any information literacy courses that are cross listed with other departments, such as computer science, psychology, history, biology, etc, or schools, such as a medical or law school? Broken Out by Total Student Enrollment

Total Student Enrollment	Yes	No
Less than 2,500	5.56%	94.44%
2.500 to 5,000	4.76%	95.24%
More than 5,000	33.33%	66.67%

Table 6.10:   Does the library offer any information literacy courses that are cross listed with other departments, such as computer science, psychology, history, biology, etc, or schools, such as a medical or law school? Broken Out by Total Number of Instruction or Presentation Sessions given by the College's Librarians in the Past Year

Number of Instruction Sessions given by College Librarians	Yes	No
Less than 100	9.52%	90.48%
100 to 200	19.05%	80.95%
More than 200	16.67%	83.33%

Table 6.11:   Which phrase best describes the attitude of upper college administrative management towards information literacy?

	I am afraid that it is not high on their agenda	They sometimes pay attention and sometimes not	It is increasingly a high priority	It is a high priority for the college
Entire Sample	31.67%	46.67%	16.67%	5.00%

Table 6.12:   Which phrase best describes the attitude of upper college administrative management towards information literacy? Broken Out by Type of College

Type of College	I am afraid that it is not high on their agenda	They sometimes pay attention and sometimes not	It is increasingly a high priority	It is a high priority for the college
Community College	25.00%	58.33%	12.50%	4.17%
4-Year College	29.41%	47.06%	17.65%	5.88%
MA or PHD Granting College	37.50%	37.50%	18.75%	6.25%
Research University	66.67%	0.00%	33.33%	0.00%

Table 6.13:   Which phrase best describes the attitude of upper college administrative management towards information literacy? Broken Out by Public or Private Status

Public or Private Status	I am afraid that it is not high on their agenda	They sometimes pay attention and sometimes not	It is increasingly a high priority	It is a high priority for the college
Public	35.00%	42.50%	17.50%	5.00%
Private	25.00%	55.00%	15.00%	5.00%

Table 6.14: Which phrase best describes the attitude of upper college administrative management towards information literacy? Broken Out by Total Student Enrollment

Total Student Enrollment	I am afraid that it is not high on their agenda	They sometimes pay attention and sometimes not	It is increasingly a high priority	It is a high priority for the college
Less than 2,500	27.78%	55.56%	11.11%	5.56%
2.500 to 5,000	33.33%	47.62%	14.29%	4.76%
More than 5,000	33.33%	38.10%	23.81%	4.76%

Table 6.15: Which phrase best describes the attitude of upper college administrative management towards information literacy? Broken Out by Total Number of Instruction or Presentation Sessions given by the College's Librarians in the Past Year

Number of Instruction Sessions given by College Librarians	I am afraid that it is not high on their agenda	They sometimes pay attention and sometimes not	It is increasingly a high priority	It is a high priority for the college
Less than 100	42.86%	42.86%	14.29%	0.00%
100 to 200	28.57%	52.38%	14.29%	4.76%
More than 200	22.22%	44.44%	22.22%	11.11%

Table 6.16: Do librarians at your institution have faculty status?

	Yes	No
Entire Sample	56.67%	43.33%

Table 6.17: Do librarians at your institution have faculty status? Broken Out by Type of College

Type of College	Yes	No
Community College	41.67%	58.33%
4-Year College	47.06%	52.94%
MA or PHD Granting College	81.25%	18.75%
Research University	100.00%	0.00%

Table 6.18: Do librarians at your institution have faculty status? Broken Out by Public or Private Status

Public or Private Status	Yes	No
Public	62.50%	37.50%
Private	45.00%	55.00%

Table 6.19: **Do librarians at your institution have faculty status? Broken Out by Total Student Enrollment**

Total Student Enrollment	Yes	No
Less than 2,500	38.89%	61.11%
2.500 to 5,000	71.43%	28.57%
More than 5,000	57.14%	42.86%

Table 6.20: **Do librarians at your institution have faculty status? Broken Out by Total Number of Instruction or Presentation Sessions given by the College's Librarians in the Past Year**

Number of Instruction Sessions given by College Librarians	Yes	No
Less than 100	38.10%	61.90%
100 to 200	66.67%	33.33%
More than 200	66.67%	33.33%

Chapter 7: Relations with the English Department

Table 7.1: Does the library send library science instructors to teach sessions to students taking the college's main English composition, rhetoric or similar required course?

	Yes	No
Entire Sample	84.21%	15.79%

Table 7.2: Does the library send library science instructors to teach sessions to students taking the college's main English composition, rhetoric or similar required course? Broken Out by Type of College

Type of College	Yes	No
Community College	82.61%	17.39%
4-Year College	81.25%	18.75%
MA or PHD Granting College	93.33%	6.67%
Research University	66.67%	33.33%

Table 7.3: Does the library send library science instructors to teach sessions to students taking the college's main English composition, rhetoric or similar required course? Broken Out by Public or Private Status

Public or Private Status	Yes	No
Public	87.18%	12.82%
Private	77.78%	22.22%

Table 7.4: Does the library send library science instructors to teach sessions to students taking the college's main English composition, rhetoric or similar required course? Broken Out by Total Student Enrollment

Total Student Enrollment	Yes	No
Less than 2,500	83.33%	16.67%
2,500 to 5,000	83.33%	16.67%
More than 5,000	85.71%	14.29%

Table 7.5: Does the library send library science instructors to teach sessions to students taking the college's main English composition, rhetoric or similar required course? Broken Out by Total Number of Instruction or Presentation Sessions given by the College's Librarians in the Past Year

Number of Instruction Sessions given by College Librarians	Yes	No
Less than 100	80.00%	20.00%
100 to 200	90.00%	10.00%
More than 200	82.35%	17.65%

Table 7.6: To what degree do library instructors make appearances in the basic composition class?

	A predetermined number of appearances	Determined by the English Department	Determined by individual composition instructors
Entire Sample	14.55%	12.73%	72.73%

Table 7.7: To what degree do library instructors make appearances in the basic composition class? Broken Out by Type of College

Type of College	A predetermined number of appearances	Determined by the English Department	Determined by individual composition instructors
Community College	17.39%	13.04%	69.57%
4-Year College	7.14%	7.14%	85.71%
MA or PHD Granting College	13.33%	13.33%	73.33%
Research University	33.33%	33.33%	33.33%

Table 7.8: To what degree do library instructors make appearances in the basic composition class? Broken Out by Public or Private Status

Public or Private Status	A predetermined number of appearances	Determined by the English Department	Determined by individual composition instructors
Public	15.79%	13.16%	71.05%
Private	11.76%	11.76%	76.47%

Table 7.9:   To what degree do library instructors make appearances in the basic composition class? Broken Out by Total Student Enrollment

Total Student Enrollment	A predetermined number of appearances	Determined by the English Department	Determined by individual composition instructors
Less than 2,500	6.25%	12.50%	81.25%
2,500 to 5,000	16.67%	11.11%	72.22%
More than 5,000	19.05%	14.29%	66.67%

Table 7.10:   To what degree do library instructors make appearances in the basic composition class? Broken Out by Total Number of Instruction or Presentation Sessions given by the College's Librarians in the Past Year

Number of Instruction Sessions given by College Librarians	A predetermined number of appearances	Determined by the English Department	Determined by individual composition instructors
Less than 100	5.26%	10.53%	84.21%
100 to 200	10.00%	15.00%	75.00%
More than 200	31.25%	12.50%	56.25%

Table 7.11:   In approximately how many three credit composition classes do library instructors make an appearance per semester?

	Mean	Median	Minimum	Maximum
Entire Sample	21.95	8.00	1.00	120.00

Table 7.12:   In approximately how many three credit composition classes do library instructors make an appearance per semester? Broken Out by Type of College

Type of College	Mean	Median	Minimum	Maximum
Community College	18.95	5.00	1.00	60.00
4-Year College	29.67	15.00	1.00	98.00
MA or PHD Granting College	19.36	12.00	1.00	120.00
Research University	18.50	18.50	2.00	35.00

Table 7.13:   In approximately how many three credit composition classes do library instructors make an appearance per semester? Broken Out by Public or Private Status

Public or Private Status	Mean	Median	Minimum	Maximum
Public	27.65	17.00	1.00	120.00
Private	8.38	3.00	1.00	50.00

Table 7.14:   In approximately how many three credit composition classes do library instructors make an appearance per semester? Broken Out by Total Student Enrollment

Total Student Enrollment	Mean	Median	Minimum	Maximum
Less than 2,500	13.50	4.50	1.00	60.00
2,500 to 5,000	14.60	10.00	1.00	43.00
More than 5,000	37.20	20.00	1.00	120.00

Table 7.15:   In approximately how many three credit composition classes do library instructors make an appearance per semester? Broken Out by Total Number of Instruction or Presentation Sessions given by the College's Librarians in the Past Year

Number of Instruction Sessions given by College Librarians	Mean	Median	Minimum	Maximum
Less than 100	10.94	5.00	1.00	50.00
100 to 200	30.56	16.00	1.00	98.00
More than 200	25.17	11.50	1.00	120.00

Table 7.16:   What is your attitude towards how the English Department carries out its information literacy responsibilities?

	Honestly we feel that they are somewhat laggard	They seem to try but they could do better	They do well enough	It is a high priority for them and they make time for us	It is an excellent collaboration and we jointly accomplish our information literacy goals
Entire Sample	10.34%	39.66%	12.07%	25.86%	12.07%

Table 7.17:   What is your attitude towards how the English Department carries out its information literacy responsibilities? Broken Out by Type of College

Type of College	Honestly we feel that they are somewhat laggard	They seem to try but they could do better	They do well enough	It is a high priority for them and they make time for us	It is an excellent collaboration and we jointly accomplish our information literacy goals
Community College	16.67%	37.50%	12.50%	25.00%	8.33%
4-Year College	6.25%	37.50%	18.75%	18.75%	18.75%
MA or PHD Granting College	6.67%	46.67%	6.67%	26.67%	13.33%
Research University	0.00%	33.33%	0.00%	66.67%	0.00%

Table 7.18:   What is your attitude towards how the English Department carries out its information literacy responsibilities? Broken Out by Public or Private Status

Public or Private Status	Honestly we feel that they are somewhat laggard	They seem to try but they could do better	They do well enough	It is a high priority for them and they make time for us	It is an excellent collaboration and we jointly accomplish our information literacy goals
Public	12.50%	30.00%	12.50%	32.50%	12.50%
Private	5.56%	61.11%	11.11%	11.11%	11.11%

Table 7.19:   What is your attitude towards how the English Department carries out its information literacy responsibilities? Broken Out by Total Student Enrollment

Total Student Enrollment	Honestly we feel that they are somewhat laggard	They seem to try but they could do better	They do well enough	It is a high priority for them and they make time for us	It is an excellent collaboration and we jointly accomplish our information literacy goals
Less than 2,500	5.88%	41.18%	17.65%	29.41%	5.88%
2,500 to 5,000	25.00%	30.00%	10.00%	25.00%	10.00%
More than 5,000	0.00%	47.62%	9.52%	23.81%	19.05%

Table 7.20: What is your attitude towards how the English Department carries out its information literacy responsibilities? Broken Out by Total Number of Instruction or Presentation Sessions given by the College's Librarians in the Past Year

Number of Instruction Sessions given by College Librarians	Honestly we feel that they are somewhat laggard	They seem to try but they could do better	They do well enough	It is a high priority for them and they make time for us	It is an excellent collaboration and we jointly accomplish our information literacy goals
Less than 100	10.00%	60.00%	15.00%	10.00%	5.00%
100 to 200	10.00%	20.00%	20.00%	30.00%	20.00%
More than 200	11.11%	38.89%	0.00%	38.89%	11.11%

Chapter 8: Interactive Tutorials

Table 8.1: Does the college offer interactive tutorials in information literacy topics to students?

	Yes	No
Entire Sample	47.46%	52.54%

Table 8.2: Does the college offer interactive tutorials in information literacy topics to students? Broken Out by Type of College

Type of College	Yes	No
Community College	37.50%	62.50%
4-Year College	52.94%	47.06%
MA or PHD Granting College	46.67%	53.33%
Research University	100.00%	0.00%

Table 8.3: Does the college offer interactive tutorials in information literacy topics to students? Broken Out by Public or Private Status

Public or Private Status	Yes	No
Public	40.00%	60.00%
Private	63.16%	36.84%

Table 8.4: Does the college offer interactive tutorials in information literacy topics to students? Broken Out by Total Student Enrollment

Total Student Enrollment	Yes	No
Less than 2,500	38.89%	61.11%
2,500 to 5,000	40.00%	60.00%
More than 5,000	61.90%	38.10%

Table 8.5: Does the college offer interactive tutorials in information literacy topics to students? Broken Out by Total Number of Instruction or Presentation Sessions given by the College's Librarians in the Past Year

Number of Instruction Sessions given by College Librarians	Yes	No
Less than 100	42.86%	57.14%
100 to 200	45.00%	55.00%
More than 200	55.56%	44.44%

Table 8.6: If the college does offer interactive tutorials in information literacy topics to students, how many such tutorials are currently offered?

	Mean	Median	Minimum	Maximum
Entire Sample	6.81	4.00	1.00	20.00

Table 8.7: If the college does offer interactive tutorials in information literacy topics to students, how many such tutorials are currently offered? Broken Out by Type of College

Type of College	Mean	Median	Minimum	Maximum
Community College	5.67	4.00	1.00	12.00
4-Year College	5.13	3.50	1.00	20.00
MA or PHD Granting College	9.71	6.00	1.00	20.00
Research University	8.00	3.00	1.00	20.00

Table 8.8: If the college does offer interactive tutorials in information literacy topics to students, how many such tutorials are currently offered? Broken Out by Public or Private Status

Public or Private Status	Mean	Median	Minimum	Maximum
Public	6.07	4.00	1.00	20.00
Private	7.75	5.00	1.00	20.00

Table 8.9: If the college does offer interactive tutorials in information literacy topics to students, how many such tutorials are currently offered? Broken Out by Total Student Enrollment

Total Student Enrollment	Mean	Median	Minimum	Maximum
Less than 2,500	4.29	4.00	1.00	12.00
2,500 to 5,000	5.75	4.50	1.00	20.00
More than 5,000	9.00	5.00	1.00	20.00

Table 8.10: If the college does offer interactive tutorials in information literacy topics to students, how many such tutorials are currently offered? Broken Out by Total Number of Instruction or Presentation Sessions given by the College's Librarians in the Past Year

Number of Instruction Sessions given by College Librarians	Mean	Median	Minimum	Maximum
Less than 100	6.67	4.00	1.00	20.00
100 to 200	8.33	5.00	1.00	20.00
More than 200	5.44	3.00	1.00	20.00

Table 8.11: Does the college offer video tutorials on information literacy topics?

	Yes	No
Entire Sample	65.52%	34.48%

Table 8.12: Does the college offer video tutorials on information literacy topics? Broken Out by Type of College

Type of College	Yes	No
Community College	58.33%	41.67%
4-Year College	75.00%	25.00%
MA or PHD Granting College	73.33%	26.67%
Research University	33.33%	66.67%

Table 8.13: Does the college offer video tutorials on information literacy topics? Broken Out by Public or Private Status

Public or Private Status	Yes	No
Public	65.00%	35.00%
Private	66.67%	33.33%

Table 8.14: Does the college offer video tutorials on information literacy topics? Broken Out by Total Student Enrollment

Total Student Enrollment	Yes	No
Less than 2,500	55.56%	44.44%
2,500 to 5,000	73.68%	26.32%
More than 5,000	66.67%	33.33%

Table 8.15:   Does the college offer video tutorials on information literacy topics? Broken Out by Total Number of Instruction or Presentation Sessions given by the College's Librarians in the Past Year

Number of Instruction Sessions given by College Librarians	Yes	No
Less than 100	61.90%	38.10%
100 to 200	75.00%	25.00%
More than 200	58.82%	41.18%

What has been the library's experience in using and making online or video-based tutorials for information literacy? Do you make you own or use those of other colleges or both? What kind of software or websites do you use to help you to make the videos or online tutorials? How do you market and distribute them?

1. Use of vendor made database tutorials
2. We have a 3-minute library overview created by Campus Media, and brief Camtasia overview of searching catalog and 2 databases
3. We make our own videos and tutorials, which are made available through BB and LibGuides
4. We make our own and link to others occasionally. I use Snagit. We don't market our videos.
5. It has been ok. We use Screencast-o-matic, because it is much cheaper than other options. Basically, the librarian in charge of instruction (me) creates a script, practices, then records a computer screen while explaining what is happening via microphone. We advertise these in the online LMS, by informing faculty, and by highlighting them in our LibGuides.
6. We have done both, made our own and used other colleges. We have used Softchalk to make an online interactive Library and Research Orientation. We have used Adobe to make the videos, and we have used LibGuides to distribute both the orientation and the videos. We market these directly to faculty through email and by attending department meetings. We also point them out to students in our IL classes.
7. We have made a few over the last year. We use Screencasting.com and Blackboard collaboration for online orientations. No marketing, upon request.
8. We are in the midst of completing out first tutorial using Adobe Capture
9. Not enough time or people to make and maintain video instruction. Occasionally post videos from other sources to the library blog.
10. We make our own. Canvas Instructure, Softchalk, Screencast-o-matic, Camtasia. Online tutorial is actually an LIB course linked to their ENGL 1301 class. They must enroll.
11. We have made our own interactive tutorial that we used in the past, but we had to remove it from our website because it was out-of-date. We have Camtasia and Media-Site and have some tutorials in both formats. They are marketed by individual classes and on our website.
12. We make our own using Camtasia, they are hosted by Screencast. They are integrated into LibGuides and our course management system, D2L. They are requested by faculty and distributed on a class by class basis.
13. We source them out. Camtasia. PR to faculty and students on website.
14. We use Jing for screen shot tutorials, web manager for HTML tutorials, and our institutional team for the videos. We link them from the library homepage and from Blackboard in several key residential and on-line classes.
15. Make our own, plus we use vendors
16. We are well versed in creating short tutorials. Most are ours but we use some through the ANTS project. Use Adobe Captivate. We mount tutorials at strategic places in our web (e.g. next to database links) and have a general Research Help link on our library home page that leads to most of our tutorials
17. We both make our own & reuse the best ones available. We prefer reusing simply because it's more sustainable. Only one librarian makes extensive use of screencasting software to record tutorials. We use Screenr or Screencast-o-matic mostly but have used Jing in the past. We post them to our YouTube account and to LibGuides. Sometimes an instructor will use them inside their course in the LMS.

18. We are too busy teaching classes to get these together. We've all tried them at one point, but the technology, course content or college curriculum changes so quickly and so often we haven't been able to keep them current enough. They also became too generalized to be useful in many cases.

19. Both. Captivate, Jing, Camtasia.

20. Make our own with Camtasia software and post on Facebook & in LibGuides

21. We do not have software or equipment for recording or editing videos

22. Have created some tutorials in past using Camtasia. No big initiative to create more - we have hired an Instructional Technologist to assist faculty with technology issues in the classroom, but so far, our requests to hire someone exclusively to develop info lit tutorials has fallen on deaf ears/no funds allocated for this initiative. Tutorials were loaded onto our library homepage and included in the LibGuides.

23, CLIP tutorials on the library tab in the Course Mgmt. System site.

24. We make our own tutorials. We use Camtasia. We put the tutorials in LibGuides on the website.

25. Make our own. Also use ones made by others, as well as those produced by database providers.

26. I make them with PowerPoint and Jing. Best practices is to make all video closed captioned.

27. Need to offer more and they are being planned

28. We have Camtasia in a limited way for online video tutorials. We make our own and also provide links to those produced in other libraries. Our tutorials are listed on our website under help.

29. Need to make many more tutorials using Camtasia and Jing, both for distance and on campus students. Need to make Camtasia interactive with Snag it. Market via faculty. List vendor tutorials on LibGuide for Tutorials.

30. We link to tutorials from CLIP and other places

31. Used Jing and Camtasia. Posted on our website and in our LibGuides. Very time-consuming to make and update.

32. We use tutorials made in house as well as some that have been created by others. This is very helpful to us. We use Camtasia to make ours and are experimenting with flash.

33. We make our own, when demonstrating a specific database or anything involving our website. But we also use other schools' tutorials and videos for quick videos to use in LI classes or in research guides. We've used Jing, Captivate, and are looking into BB Collaborate and Panopto.

34. Both: We use Voice Thread, Adobe Captivate, mostly. We promote them to our individual faculty who add them to their BlackBoard courses.

35. Both. Via our web pages.

36. Still in the testing phase, as our tutorials are made by the database providers and I embed the code of the tutorials into our LibGuides. I am looking into purchasing a small subscription to purchasing Jing and creating school specific videos for better tutorials. We market using LibGuides. The HTMLs are posted on the library website, on our student portal, during the seminars, and on the monitors of the library computers.

37. Captivate. YouTube. Use in house and from others.

38. We are in the process of developing such tools for our students

39. Make our own, available on LibGuides

40. We make our own. They are housed on the library's website.

41. We use Screencast-o-matic. Post the videos with our subject guide. Starting to record adobe connect sessions - so far not making that link available to anyone other than the faculty & class involved.

42. We use Captivate and have used Camtasia. Also Jing for quick-and-dirty video. We generally make our own but have adapted our plagiarism tutorial from another library.

43. Video-based tutorials are very time consuming to create, and they need frequent updating. Online tutorials are much easier to create and maintain.

44. Videos on specific search/research techniques. On library webpages for specific departments/programs/subjects.

45. We have online material explaining how to use the catalog and databases, but have not branched out into more complex information literacy topics

46. We do some of both. We have used Camtasia and linked to YouTube, and they are generally incorporated into LibGuides.

47. The college has recently hired an Instructional Designer. The library is working with him to create video based and online tutorials via the library website.

Table 8.16:   If the library offers interactive tutorials over the web, how many unique visits does the tutorial page receive on a typical month when college is in session?

	Mean	Median	Minimum	Maximum
Entire Sample	1183.90	145.00	4.00	10000.00

Table 8.17:   If the library offers interactive tutorials over the web, how many unique visits does the tutorial page receive on a typical month when college is in session? Broken Out by Public or Private Status

Public or Private Status	Mean	Median	Minimum	Maximum
Public	148.00	190.00	50.00	200.00
Private	2219.80	50.00	4.00	10000.00

Table 8.18:   If the library offers interactive tutorials over the web, how many unique visits does the tutorial page receive on a typical month when college is in session? Broken Out by Total Student Enrollment

Total Student Enrollment	Mean	Median	Minimum	Maximum
Less than 2,500	51.33	50.00	4.00	100.00
2,500 to 5,000	98.33	50.00	45.00	200.00
More than 5,000	2847.50	600.00	190.00	10000.00

Table 8.19:   If the library offers interactive tutorials over the web, how many unique visits does the tutorial page receive on a typical month when college is in session? Broken Out by Total Number of Instruction or Presentation Sessions given by the College's Librarians in the Past Year

Number of Instruction Sessions given by College Librarians	Mean	Median	Minimum	Maximum
Less than 100	33.00	45.00	4.00	50.00
100 to 200	1925.00	200.00	50.00	10000.00
More than 200	190.00	190.00	190.00	190.00

*Not enough information to calculate the number of unique visits received by tutorial pages broken out by type of college

Chapter 9: Instructional Lab

Table 9.1: Does the library have one or more instructional labs or learning centers designed for information literacy instruction in which much of the library's formal information literacy instruction takes place?

	Yes	No
Entire Sample	55.93%	44.07%

Table 9.2: Does the library have one or more instructional labs or learning centers designed for information literacy instruction in which much of the library's formal information literacy instruction takes place? Broken Out by Type of College

Type of College	Yes	No
Community College	58.33%	41.67%
4-Year College	41.18%	58.82%
MA or PHD Granting College	66.67%	33.33%
Research University	66.67%	33.33%

Table 9.3: Does the library have one or more instructional labs or learning centers designed for information literacy instruction in which much of the library's formal information literacy instruction takes place? Broken Out by Public or Private Status

Public or Private Status	Yes	No
Public	65.00%	35.00%
Private	36.84%	63.16%

Table 9.4: Does the library have one or more instructional labs or learning centers designed for information literacy instruction in which much of the library's formal information literacy instruction takes place? Broken Out by Total Student Enrollment

Total Student Enrollment	Yes	No
Less than 2,500	50.00%	50.00%
2,500 to 5,000	60.00%	40.00%
More than 5,000	57.14%	42.86%

Table 9.5: Does the library have one or more instructional labs or learning centers designed for information literacy instruction in which much of the library's formal information literacy instruction takes place? Broken Out by Total Number of Instruction or Presentation Sessions given by the College's Librarians in the Past Year

Number of Instruction Sessions given by College Librarians	Yes	No
Less than 100	38.10%	61.90%
100 to 200	60.00%	40.00%
More than 200	72.22%	27.78%

Table 9.6: If the library has one or more instructional labs or learning centers designed for information literacy instruction, how many seats or individual workstations do these centers offer in total?

	Mean	Median	Minimum	Maximum
Entire Sample	42.60	30.00	0.00	157.00

Table 9.7: If the library has one or more instructional labs or learning centers designed for information literacy instruction, how many seats or individual workstations do these centers offer in total? Broken Out by Type of College

Type of College	Mean	Median	Minimum	Maximum
Community College	29.53	25.00	0.00	60.00
4-Year College	35.71	28.00	18.00	70.00
MA or PHD Granting College	49.18	30.00	25.00	116.00
Research University	128.50	128.50	100.00	157.00

Table 9.8: If the library has one or more instructional labs or learning centers designed for information literacy instruction, how many seats or individual workstations do these centers offer in total? Broken Out by Public or Private Status

Public or Private Status	Mean	Median	Minimum	Maximum
Public	43.63	30.00	0.00	157.00
Private	39.13	30.00	12.00	100.00

Table 9.9: If the library has one or more instructional labs or learning centers designed for information literacy instruction, how many seats or individual workstations do these centers offer in total? Broken Out by Total Student Enrollment

Total Student Enrollment	Mean	Median	Minimum	Maximum
Less than 2,500	31.60	33.00	0.00	60.00
2,500 to 5,000	28.42	24.50	16.00	50.00
More than 5,000	64.15	50.00	25.00	157.00

Table 9.10: If the library has one or more instructional labs or learning centers designed for information literacy instruction, how many seats or individual workstations do these centers offer in total? Broken Out by Total Number of Instruction or Presentation Sessions given by the College's Librarians in the Past Year

Number of Instruction Sessions given by College Librarians	Mean	Median	Minimum	Maximum
Less than 100	28.44	30.00	0.00	52.00
100 to 200	43.54	30.00	20.00	100.00
More than 200	51.46	34.00	18.00	157.00

Table 9.11: What percentage of the time when college is in full session is the center in use by any party including by non-library instructors?

	Mean	Median	Minimum	Maximum
Entire Sample	48.13	47.50	5.00	100.00

Table 9.12: What percentage of the time when college is in full session is the center in use by any party including by non-library instructors? Broken Out by Type of College

Type of College	Mean	Median	Minimum	Maximum
Community College	47.31	50.00	15.00	100.00
4-Year College	45.71	50.00	5.00	85.00
MA or PHD Granting College	52.50	37.50	5.00	100.00
Research University	40.00	40.00	10.00	70.00

Table 9.13:   What percentage of the time when college is in full session is the center in use by any party including by non-library instructors? Broken Out by Public or Private Status

Public or Private Status	Mean	Median	Minimum	Maximum
Public	49.60	45.00	5.00	100.00
Private	42.86	50.00	5.00	80.00

Table 9.14:   What percentage of the time when college is in full session is the center in use by any party including by non-library instructors? Broken Out by Total Student Enrollment

Total Student Enrollment	Mean	Median	Minimum	Maximum
Less than 2,500	57.22	60.00	5.00	100.00
2,500 to 5,000	34.09	30.00	5.00	60.00
More than 5,000	54.17	52.50	10.00	100.00

Table 9.15:   What percentage of the time when college is in full session is the center in use by any party including by non-library instructors? Broken Out by Total Number of Instruction or Presentation Sessions given by the College's Librarians in the Past Year

Number of Instruction Sessions given by College Librarians	Mean	Median	Minimum	Maximum
Less than 100	64.29	80.00	5.00	100.00
100 to 200	41.67	40.00	10.00	100.00
More than 200	45.38	50.00	5.00	85.00

Table 9.16:   How many years ago was the center constructed or significantly remodeled?

	Mean	Median	Minimum	Maximum
Entire Sample	6.43	5.00	0.50	16.00

Table 9.17:   How many years ago was the center constructed or significantly remodeled? Broken Out by Type of College

Type of College	Mean	Median	Minimum	Maximum
Community College	5.38	3.50	1.00	12.00
4-Year College	8.83	8.50	1.00	16.00
MA or PHD Granting College	5.50	5.50	0.50	12.00
Research University	8.00	8.00	8.00	8.00

Table 9.18:   How many years ago was the center constructed or significantly remodeled? Broken Out by Public or Private Status

Public or Private Status	Mean	Median	Minimum	Maximum
Public	6.50	7.00	0.50	16.00
Private	6.31	4.00	0.50	15.00

Table 9.19:   How many years ago was the center constructed or significantly remodeled? Broken Out by Total Student Enrollment

Total Student Enrollment	Mean	Median	Minimum	Maximum
Less than 2,500	8.43	7.00	2.00	16.00
2,500 to 5,000	5.57	5.00	0.50	12.00
More than 5,000	5.56	4.00	1.00	12.00

Table 9.20:   How many years ago was the center constructed or significantly remodeled? Broken Out by Total Number of Instruction or Presentation Sessions given by the College's Librarians in the Past Year

Number of Instruction Sessions given by College Librarians	Mean	Median	Minimum	Maximum
Less than 100	6.08	5.50	0.50	12.00
100 to 200	5.39	4.00	0.50	12.00
More than 200	7.88	7.50	1.00	16.00

Table 9.21: Which phrase best describes the level of investment in equipment, space, software and other aids to teach information literacy and related subjects the library will makes over the next three years?

	Increase significantly	Increase somewhat	Remain about the same	Decline somewhat	Decline precipitously
Entire Sample	14.55%	29.09%	50.91%	1.82%	3.64%

Table 9.22: Which phrase best describes the level of investment in equipment, space, software and other aids to teach information literacy and related subjects the library will makes over the next three years? Broken Out by Type of College

Type of College	Increase significantly	Increase somewhat	Remain about the same	Decline somewhat	Decline precipitously
Community College	0.00%	34.78%	56.52%	4.35%	4.35%
4-Year College	25.00%	31.25%	37.50%	0.00%	6.25%
MA or PHD Granting College	28.57%	21.43%	50.00%	0.00%	0.00%
Research University	0.00%	0.00%	100.00%	0.00%	0.00%

Table 9.23: Which phrase best describes the level of investment in equipment, space, software and other aids to teach information literacy and related subjects the library will makes over the next three years? Broken Out by Public or Private Status

Public or Private Status	Increase significantly	Increase somewhat	Remain about the same	Decline somewhat	Decline precipitously
Public	10.26%	28.21%	53.85%	2.56%	5.13%
Private	25.00%	31.25%	43.75%	0.00%	0.00%

Table 9.24: Which phrase best describes the level of investment in equipment, space, software and other aids to teach information literacy and related subjects the library will makes over the next three years? Broken Out by Total Student Enrollment

Total Student Enrollment	Increase significantly	Increase somewhat	Remain about the same	Decline somewhat	Decline precipitously
Less than 2,500	16.67%	33.33%	38.89%	5.56%	5.56%
2,500 to 5,000	11.11%	33.33%	55.56%	0.00%	0.00%
More than 5,000	15.79%	21.05%	57.89%	0.00%	5.26%

Table 9.25: Which phrase best describes the level of investment in equipment, space, software and other aids to teach information literacy and related subjects the library will makes over the next three years? Broken Out by Total Number of Instruction or Presentation Sessions given by the College's Librarians in the Past Year

Number of Instruction Sessions given by College Librarians	Increase significantly	Increase somewhat	Remain about the same	Decline somewhat	Decline precipitously
Less than 100	15.79%	26.32%	52.63%	0.00%	5.26%
100 to 200	20.00%	30.00%	40.00%	5.00%	5.00%
More than 200	6.25%	31.25%	62.50%	0.00%	0.00%

Chapter 10: Favored Resources

Please mention some of the resources that you have used in designing and maintaining your information literacy program. Please mention valued websites, listservs, blogs, books, monographs, journals, databases, tutorials, newsletters, magazines, ezines, conferences and other favored resources.

1. Primo, Merlot, ala publications
2. GA International Conf on IL, LOEX Conference, LOEX Quarterly, Portal: Libraries and the Academy Reference Services Review, Library Science and Information Technology Index
3. ILI
4. ILI listserv, ACRL
5. ProQuest, EBSCOhost, RefWorks, Westlaw
6. We have a committee in Florida for the LIS2004 (Intro to Internet Research) class that serves as the main information literacy source. That class also helps us to prepare the one-shot instruction, though we also stay current with articles in the ACRL publications and various blogs.
7. ILI listserv, CLIP, LISTA, LibGuide community pages, Computers in Libraries
8. Mainly we use our website, Purdue OWL and handouts
9. ILI listserv, LOEX, www.calstatela.edu/library/research/, www.calstatela.edu/library/tutorials.htm, www.calstatela.edu/library/guides/pswhat.htm, www.library.vanderbilt.edu/peabody/tutorials/scholarlyfree/
10. This question seems a bit overwhelming. In addition to reading broadly, deeply, and frequently about info literacy, I also read quite a bit about critical thinking and research. No favorite resource springs to mind. It's all about picking bits and pieces that will work best for our students and within the particular constraints of this library.
11. WILU, LOEX, Educause
12. ALA Conference, ACRL Conference, LibGuides, CJC-L discussion list. Books: Let the Games Begin - Neal Schuman (full disclosure - I have 2 items in the book, but I have used others), Student Engagement Techniques: A Handbook for College Faculty, Library Instruction Cookbook, ANTS tutorials sometimes
13. We are now using LibGuides as a major resources. We use a lot of EBSCO databases, WorldCat Local, OhioLINK, OhioLINK's EJC, RefWorks, and other appropriate sources, depending on the class.
14. ACRL Immersion, LOEX Conference, ACRL Instruction Section, Effective Teaching Reflective Learning book, ACRL standards, AAC&U value rubrics, RAILS rubric, Communications in Information Literacy,
15. Credo/Literati
16. We used ALA and ACRL publications and email lists. We also visited and talked with peer institutions.
17. Tutorials from Coastal Carolina Community College are great
18. Tutorials, LibGuides, blogs, newsletters
19. We use the textbook, William Badke, Research Strategies: Finding your Way through the Information Fog as a textbook. ALA Information Literacy Listserv. We generally follow key journals to keep up on the topic.
20. Kimbel Library has the best videos: http://vimeo.com/user4133833. I've also enjoyed LIONTV: https://www.youtube.com/user/1LIONTV. Finally, PRIMO: http://www.ala.org/CFApps/Primo/public/search2.cfm. Books, blogs, newsletters, etc. are mostly worthless on this level. It's more valuable to see what our student use, what they find confusing, then respond to their needs.
21. Most of our efforts go here: http://www.cord.edu/Academics/Library/instruction1.php. We also use things like SurveyMonkey, Prezi, some online video creation tools, etc. But, we do so as individual instructors. I've tried to use the LOEX site, but haven't found it as helpful as I might like. Organization isn't great and it's become kind of large and unwieldy. YouTube has a few things in it. But, I like making up my own questionnaires and active learning exercises so that they can be geared directly to our collection and the students' assignments. Google sites is our web creation tool of choice at the moment.

22. Meetings, creating LibGuides, promotion of our resources via student newspaper, exhibits and collaboration with faculty. Increasingly meeting with faculty at beginning of semesters to hand out bookmarks, information sheets and ask that faculty add us as course builders onto their Blackboard pages. We added a library link last year to each faculty's Bb page. Our book and magazine budget has declined in favor of increased monies for e-books (consortial arrangement) and database access for journals. We are allocated a certain amount (each librarian) to attend professional conferences to stay current and encouraged to present or publish even there is no incentive to do so (no tenure/faculty status accorded librarians @ this institution.)

23. CLIP tutorials, LibGuides, YouTube, Distance Ed conferences

24. Reflective Teaching, Effective Learning by Char Booth, ACRL Immersion Program

25. All the above mentioned items

26. I'm the only one on the Library staff who takes an interest in this. I've used Jing to make training tutorials. The other 2.5 staff members maintain the physical library. I give class presentations upon request.

27. Most of our "literacy program" is wishful thinking right now

28. I value Phil Bradley's website for introducing me to new search engines, and the Purdue Owl website for authoritative information on citation formats

29. Our session are held mostly the library in computer labs so we rely heavily on electronic resources such as databases and our shared library catalog

30. ACRL Immersion, ACRL publications, conferences, RSR, Comm in IL. JAL, JIL, LILAC, Sheila Webber's blog, Barbara Fister's blog

31. We have used the SAILS test to benchmark our students' skills; we developed an online Information Literacy Quiz that is taken after view in the online tutorials

32. Library news feeds, campus calendars and newspapers, notices to individual departments, personal emails

33. YouTube!

34. Softchalk, LibGuides

35. ILI-l listserv, TEDtalks, Practical pedagogy for library instructors: 17 innovative strategies to improve student learning, Metrolina Information Literacy Conference

36. We focus on principles rather than specific sites. While each library faculty member uses a single syllabus, each library faculty member has his/her own approach to that syllabus. Approaches vary widely.

37. OWL, NoodleTools

38. Tutorials by the database providers, listserv, viewing other school websites and LibGuides, ALA, and interdepartmental activities

39. Big6, ACRL

40. Our Pot of Gold Tutorial: http://www.library.nd.edu/instruction/potofgold/

41. OhioLINK resources, Google Scholar, Academic Search complete and other databases. LibGuides are written by our instruction librarian.

42. Pbwiki, Screencast-o-matic, Adobe Connect, Ustream, ALA listservs, PaLA & ALA conferences

43. ILI-L, Infolit-l, Rusa-l, Ebss-l, ACRL. Conferences: ALA, WILU, LOEX of the West. Two of us have attended Information Literacy Institute. Books such as "Make it visual in the classroom" about visual language processing. Too many to list or think of here.

44. Tables in library in library classroom that have built-in recesses for laptop-computers. We can now use room as standard non-computer classroom with tables closed or open tables and have a hard wired computer classroom.

45. I have used the CJC-l listserv and a variety of books on teaching library tutorials and creating information literacy assignments. However, what we offer in terms of information literacy probably does not add up to a "program" as such.

46. My dissertation, WPA list

What role have social media sites such as Twitter and Facebook and video aggregation sites (such as YouTube and Vimeo) played in your information literacy efforts?

1. Somewhat. Promotion of resources on Facebook and Twitter.
2. Facebook is used to promote the library, make announcements, and share industry trends
3. Social media sites are used as instructional aids
4. None
5. We use Vimeo but no social media sites
6. We host our videos on YouTube (there is no server space at the college for the files) and advertise new LibGuides on Twitter. Otherwise, our students are not very engaged in college-sponsored social media.
7. YouTube plays a big role. Facebook and Twitter no role at all.
8. None
9. Very little. Occasionally a video on YouTube will make it to the library blog.
10. It has played a valuable role, and is consulted and used daily
11. YouTube (sometimes Vimeo) - incorporate videos in my teaching sessions
12. We have used some YouTube videos. We use Twitter and Facebook to market library programs, but not for actual instruction.
13. None, we have a library Facebook page but it is not connected to information literacy efforts
14. Will in the future
15. We are starting a video channel with more than 400 screen-shot tutorials. We are announcing them on the Library Facebook page.
16. Twitter is an active part of the library effort. Facebook is too. We also have a blog.
17. YouTube video
18. YouTube for uploading tutorials
19. We sometimes distribute materials or information through Facebook or Twitter but have little evidence that it has any effect. YouTube, on the other hand, is a vital distribution mechanism. It is free hosting and makes embedding on any platform (e.g. mobile-friendly) easy. Instructors can grab embed codes easily. We can favorite and reuse others' videos easily. We can centralize our tutorials and group them into subject areas. It is easily the best distribution platform for videos. Libraries that do this manually on their own site are making a foolish mistake.
20. Not huge. We have a site for the library and a Twitter account, but our students don't really use them. Our campus uses Moodle as the online course software and so our library course pages (see above) can easily be linked there. Many of our faculty members have come to rely on these pages.
21. Very little
22. No Twitter, We have a Facebook presence, but no specific person is assigned to post there. Catch as catch can. We are short staffed even as information literacy classes are being requested more and more in light of our new Research accreditation initiative to imbed more research initiatives into the curriculum.
23. Small role
24. Sometime we advertise instruction opportunities through social media
25. None
26. Use YouTube to show how to evaluate sources
27. Very little
28. Have linked to some YouTube videos but haven't used other social media extensively
29. Not much yet
30. We are developing a YouTube channel for technology and instructional videos
31. Currently less than 5% of inquiries to libraries for access to collections/services
32. None
33. We have a Facebook account
34. I follow a few library blogs and keep track of new videos on TEDtalks, but I don't use Twitter or Facebook for work
35. A couple of us use Twitter for reminders, emphasizing key points in lessons, etc.
36. Just beginning
37. No role yet
38. To bring home the message of being Information Literate, I use a lot of Videos from YouTube

39. We list workshops on Facebook
40. Our instruction librarian includes video sources including YouTube in her LibGuides and classes as appropriate
41. Minimal
42. Not much yet
43. None up to now. We are beginning to use Kaltura (intranet video channel).
44. They've played a limited role to date
45. None! We lack the number of staff to do daily monitoring of Facebook and don't have enough interesting or relevant to say on Twitter to do it well. I will not establish a service if we can't consistently do it well. We have used YouTube for some videos and have used Flicker for photos, but do not maintain a constantly updated presence.
46. None
47. A small role
48. Use YouTube and Vimeo in some sessions

‑‑T‑

Made in the USA
Lexington, KY
16 April 2013